R. Freda

KUNDALINI YOGA *for* STRENGTH, SUCCESS, & SPIRIT

❖◆❖

Ravi Singh

White Lion Press

225 E. 5th St. #4D

New York, New York 10003

ISBN 0-9615707-2-5

Library of Congress Catalog Card Number 91-65197

Distributed by:

New Leaf
5425 Tulane Dr. SW
Atlanta, GA 30336

Bookpeople
2929 5th St.
Berkeley, CA 94710

Deep Books
81 Oakleigh Avenue
Edgware, Middlesex HA8 5DS
England

G.T. International
1800 S. Robertson Suite 182
Los Angeles, CA 90035

Contents

SPECIAL THANKS:
Dr. Dharma Singh Khalsa M.D., Carmel Zucker, Deborah Mays,
Gurucharan Singh Khalsa Ph.D, Gurudarshan Kaur Khalsa,
Thomas G. Unterburger, Gloria Bender, and Siri Vishnu Singh Khalsa

PHOTOGRAPHY & ILLUSTRATIONS
Cover photograph: Yuseff
Frontispiece: Raphael Freida, 1914
Illustrations: Ram Das Kaur (Silvestri)
Demonstrators: Ram Das Kaur, Siri Vishnu Singh Khalsa
Photographs accompanying text: Carmel Zucker
Back cover photograph: Monica Hayes

DESIGN
Design and typography: Thomas G. Unterburger
Text face: Kennerly; Headings: Nicolas Cochin Bold

DISCLAIMER
This book is a reference work and should ideally be used under
the auspices of a qualified Teacher of Kundalini Yoga. This book is not
necessarily meant to be used in lieu of professional medical
or psychological care for the treatment of any outstanding condition.

*This book is lovingly dedicated
to Yogi Bhajan
whose example, sacrifice, and Wisdom
have made this work possible.*

PLANTING THE SEEDS OF DISCIPLINE

*T*he inner prompting for self-discovery, self-improvement, and the deep desire to connect with something beyond oneself, are intrinsic to the human experience.

The key word here is experience. There are myriads of self-appointed experts on all manner of things psychological and mystical. It's a common human foible to think that knowledge of something somehow exonerates one from the practical and necessary work involved.

So, it's one thing to read endless books on philosophy, spirituality, and self-motivation; in fact, this may constitute an important first step. But the real results come to those who honestly work on themselves, systematically and consciously.

Work on oneself starts with the realization that "There must be something more," or "I'm in pain and want to heal myself and my life." Then a technology is needed to reprogram and reenergize oneself. As we recover from the pain of the past it becomes easier to improve the quality of our lives.

It could be said that the pursuit of happiness is a physiological process. In order to realize our full potential, maintain a positive outlook, and insulate ourselves against the stresses of the times, a healthy glandular system, strong nervous system, and a reassessment and repatterning of one's behavior are essential. Kundalini Yoga fulfills these requirements.

In addition, Kundalini Yoga works with models of energy flow and frequency which reflect and enhance the entire range of human expression, understanding, and potential.

In this work our mind and body become the laboratory, our Awareness the scientist, and Spirit the open-ended grant which makes great discoveries imminent.

SPIRIT

You are fire engines
Of accelerated time
In cities of the
World to come,
The indefatigable
Insomnia
Of the soul,
A conflagration on the keyboard
Of the spine,
The climb to sun
Of fever poinsettias,
And the propaganda of their hues,
You are the lighter; my life is a fuse.

You exist in us to lead us
To the promise we made
To ourselves,
And fulfillment
Of that promise,
The easement of fears,
And an end to this imperial pain;
And with every conscious act
We draw a line,
On the blueprint
For a body of light,
And something quickens
When nothing
Out of the ordinary occurs,
Something inviolate and pure.
We hear Supreme Music
Inside the walls of space,
And the argent sun-filled air
Is awash
With the invisible snowfall Grace.

–Ravi Singh

CHAPTER 1

SPIRIT RISING

*And in the Emptiness where I raise you
I will open the roadway of lightning,
And utter the greatest exclamation
A man ever attempted.*

–Yves Bonnefoy

KUNDALINI

A scientist might call it the basic bio-energy of our being, a psychologist, the motivating factor within us, a Baptist, the Holy Ghost, an anthropologist, a Universal archetype in the growth of the psyche. Yogi Bhajan has defined Kundalini as "That which enables us to experience Infinity in the finite."

However you care to define it, Kundalini empowers us to be humanly human and Divinely inspired, and to shine, prosper, and excel in all things. Thus, through whatever means, and under whatever label, Kundalini is the common denominator for all forms of self-healing, inspiration, and transformation.

THE PROCESS OF KUNDALINI

According to Yoga, the pineal gland, to a large extent, stops secreting around age eight. As a result a certain radiance goes out of our personality, along with a capacity for Innocence and Universality. A kind of cosmic amnesia sets in.

In order to rekindle our creative potential as adults, energy must be gathered at the solar plexus so that a charge can activate Kundalini energy "sleeping" at the base of the spine. Through conscious work on oneself, higher gland functions are stimulated and the Awareness which is our birthright is reinstated.

YOGA

The word "yoga" originated with the Sanskrit word for yoke. Through the process of yoga, we want to yoke ourselves to our Higher Selves.

There are many kinds of Yoga, each of which is suited to a temperment and level of development. All of these systems have much to offer and will probably serve to enhance your experience of Kundalini Yoga.

For our purposes, let's equate the word Yoga with balance. Balance is intrinsic to everything. Kundalini Yoga will help you maintain your balance in life and compensate for all the stressful influences which constantly threaten to upset your equilibrium.

Through this work, we want to participate fully in life from the perspective of our inner life. We want to build our Awareness to encompass here and hereafter and dance across the tightrope of Time.

Historical Context

Kundalini is called the "Mother of All Yogas" because it is the original system present-day systems owe their ancestry.

According to the Yogic paradigm, mankind has devolved from a time of Great Enlightenment (The Golden Age) when Kundalini Yoga was openly taught and practiced, to present history called Kali Yug (The Dark Age), when technologies such as Kundalini Yoga are no longer widely understood or practiced.

Throughout the cathartic upheavals of the past 4,000 years, Teachers of Truth have consistently appeared in times of greatest need and shared the technology of Spirit unqualifiedly.

The Universal Knowledge shared by these exalted Teachers has been called Sanatan Dharma (the Eternal Way). One great Saint who has been seen in the context of this tradition was Guru Nanak (b. 1469) who, although having become acquainted with many ascetic practices, felt that Yoga should enhance one's life in the human community and that the relationship between an individual and the Infinite is a birthright and needs no intermediary.

It was in the tradition and spirit of sharing shown by Guru Nanak and through Guru Ram Das (fourth in the lineage of ten Gurus and "King of the Yogis"), that Yogi Bhajan (see page 158) came to the United States in 1969 to teach Kundalini Yoga to all. Kundalini Yoga is an important tool as humanity gains momentum and begins to come full circle in its evolution towards collective Higher Consciousness.

Kundalini Yoga

Kundalini Yoga combines breathing, movement, meditation, stretching, relaxation, the science of sequence, and rhythm and sound, to work on every aspect of your body, mind, and being. No previous experience in yoga or related disciplines is required for you to begin to achieve undeniable benefits almost immediately.

Kundalini Yoga is not your typical pantheon of pretty poses. The discipline is an active one, with emphasis on results. Accordingly, it deals a body/mind/spirit plan for the 90s and beyond.

Consider making this technology an intrinsic part of your life. I guarantee you that in a very short time, you'll be hard pressed to imagine how you ever got along without it!

As you practice Kundalini Yoga over time, certain physiological prerequisites are met for total health and to facilitate your transformation. These include a balanced glandular system, strong nervous system, expanded lung capacity, and the erradication of emotional blocks that manifest as holding patterns in the musculature.

The process we promulgate is graceful and gradual. We're not looking for inner fireworks or "miracles." To those of us who've practiced and prospered through this work, the greatest miracle of all, in retrospect, was being given the opportunity to walk a path with heart such as this.

When you take this system to heart, your life becomes consecrated to the process of expansion and growth. You will literally come to feel you've awakened from a bad dream and that a beautiful day is beckoning. Your most powerful aspect, once dormant as a dessicated seed, will blossom in the light and air of Awareness, your creative potential will be realized, and you will live in the effulgence of an experience no words can encompass.

THIS BOOK

This book will address basic human issues and needs and offer elegant and original approaches for mental and physical fitness and finesse in life. Much information regarding the physiological and spiritual implications of this work will be presented, but the emphasis will be on your personal experience.

Because Kundalini Yoga is the kind of thing one eventually wants to do every day, many people have expressed the desire for variance in workout times and content. I have organized this book in a way that will allow for a certain amount of creativity in designing the length and content of your workouts, while maintaining the integrity of the synergistic effect that Kundalini Yoga routines engender.

Chapter 2

Body, Mind & Being

Some Models

Kundalini Yoga recognizes and works with specific interrelated aspects, both material and sublime, of the body/mind/being construct. Some of these are:

Body

This has been fashioned under the influence of nutrition, prenatal care, and early experiences (such as the trauma of birth and initial bonding or lack of it). The general blueprint for one's physical makeup is determined at a very young age. It is the "set" of the nervous system, which doesn't change readily, but can be accommodated nicely.

Meridians

Meridians are flows of energy along certain lines in the body. These are qualities of energy, the grosser manifestation of which are the organs. Working with these energies brings balance and healing. Acupuncture is based on this model.

Qualities of Energy

An important yogic paradigm recognizes qualities of energy in the body (vayus). The most important of these energies are prana and apana. Prana, an expanding energy, relates to the lungs and the upper body. Apana, a downward or eliminating energy, relates to the lower body.

A surplus of prana makes us overly hyper, a surplus of apana too lethargic. For optimum health, prana and apana must be in balance. These two energies meet and combine at the solar plexus.

MIND

This is the playground of our biological and instinctual self. It has the blended characteristics of all the senses, and represents the cognitive strategies we use to experience, survive, and hopefully thrive in our world. This level can be transformed very powerfully from the perspective of the third level.

HIGHER COGNITION (SPIRIT)

This level is actually beyond the mind (time and space) and thus timeless. From this level we can appreciate ourselves in our totality and transform the mundane into the Miraculous.

CHAKRAS

The word Chakra means wheel. Chakras are spinning vortices of energy at important nerve or gland junctures along the spine. Each Chakra relates to a specific frequency of our capability and caliber. We want to allow for the free flow of energy throughout these centers so as to be able to bring the appropriate behavior and expression to any given situation and thus consistently excel. See Appendix 1 for a description of the Chakras.

SUBTLE ENERGY FLOWS

Yogic science has mapped a series of subtle energy flows which parallel the nervous system, called Nadis. The three most important of these are housed by the spine. They are the Ida, Pingala, and Shushuma, which can be said to be negative, positive, and neutral. When the negative and positive energies come into balance, they blend and rise up the central channel so that Spirit, in its chrysalis of time and space, can spread its wings, and drink the ambrosial nectar in the Garden of Grace!

THE TEN BODIES

These are aspects of your totality in a multidimensional sense. They are: Soul Body; Negative, Positive, and Neutral Mind; Physical Body; Arcline, Magnetic Field; Pranic Body; Subtle Body; and Radiant Body. See Appendix 2 for a description of each of the Ten Bodies.

THE MAGNETIC FIELD

The Magnetic Field (one of the Ten Bodies) is the energetic emanation of the nervous system. According to Yoga, when the Magnetic Field is strong we have radiance and charisma, and are insulated against negativity and mishap.

In certain contexts of Kundalini Yoga, we work on circulation and the nerves to strengthen the Magnetic Field. At other times, we stimulate the Magnetic Field to work on specific energy centers or systems of the body.

THE SPINE

The body can be considered an energy grid with the spine as main transformer. Kundalini Yoga acknowledges the importance of the spine and employs many techniques that work on it directly.

The spine is where many of the models discussed here interface. Any chiropractor can tell you that the spine, as the conduit for the central nervous system, has a tie-in to every system and organ.

The spine is a spectrum of frequencies (the Chakras), the sum of which comprises our totality. In addition, the spine acts as a conveyance for Kundalini energy itself, which activates these frequencies so that we can flourish in all areas of life.

BIOCHEMICAL MODEL

Our brains and bodies are regulated by an ocean of chemicals. At present at least sixty (with more being classified all the time) known neuropeptides are released in us under various circumstances. These substances are a bridge between our gross and subtle anatomy. Each of these has a salubrious and/or stimulating effect on us. The most well known of the peptides are the endorphines.

Endorphines have been linked to various heightened mood states, including the phenomena known as "runners' high," and the "afterglow" people frequently experience subsequent to sex. Endorphines and other peptides are also responsible for modulating such important physiological functions as pain suppression and immune system enhancement.

Yogis, Saints, and Sages have spent centuries perfecting various spiritual exercises as a catalyst towards specific effects. What has been traditionally termed "nectar" by Yogis is the hormonal secretion produced by the hypothalmus, pineal, and pituitary glands.

The endorphines released by these go throughout the body to decrease pain, reduce inflamation, accelerate healing and are a factor in combatting depression. In the brain, they have the effect of improving mood, attitude, and behavior.

Kundalini Yoga triggers the release of biochemical substrates through its various sequences of exercises, breath techniques, mantras, positions, and locks, in exactly the right proportions to engender specific states of elevated consciousness.

CHAPTER 3

ON YOUR MARK, GET SET...

BASIC COMPONENTS
OF KUNDALINI YOGA

BREATH

Breath is the Kiss of Power, a Gift of Grace, the love-seat swing where the finite and Infinite embrace, water from the well of Life. In other words, it's a conveyance for life force, which in Yogic parlance is termed Prana.

Breathing also has psychological implications. Yoga holds that breath is a surfboard for the subtle energies of the mind. A particular mood, feeling, or thought is always accompanied by a corresponding breath with a specific rate and quality. By learning to monitor and control our breathing, we can have a greater degree of control over our mental and emotional states, and effectiveness in life.

Unless otherwise specified, all breathing in this book is done through the nose only, on both the inhale and exhale.

LONG DEEP BREATHING

The key to Long Deep Breathing is in allowing yourself to relax. As you inhale, let the diaphragm, sides of the ribs, lower back, and stomach expand. Exhale, pulling the navel in gently as the air is evenly and completely expelled.

LONG LIGHT BREATHING

Long Light Breathing can bring calmness and clarity in just minutes. It might help to have the underside of the tongue on the roof of the mouth (this not only completes an important energy circuit, but also helps to restrict the flow of the breath to keep it long). Long Light Breathing is not raspy; it's smooth, audible only to the breather.

Most people breath between 10 and 15 times a minute. If you can get this down to eight times or less it will make you intuitive and relaxed. In certain Yogic writings long light breathing is described as "thread-like."

BREATH OF FIRE

Breath of Fire is a rapid, rhythmic breath through the nose, which puts an equal emphasis on the inhale and exhale. It resembles sniffing. Because of the rhythmic nature of this breath, everything from the neck down involves itself. A kind of bellows effect is created.

Breath of Fire creates a rhythmic entrainment among all systems and organs (and thus puts you in sync with yourself), purifies and oxygenates the blood (supplying an aerobic effect while allowing the heart to stay relaxed), raises the voltage of the nervous system, remagnetizes the cells, and engenders an optimum brain-wave balance. In addition, Breath of Fire can give you the internal effects in a pose or exercise—in just one minute—which would have taken upwards of an hour breathing at a normal rate.

If you live in an urban area where air pollution is a negative factor, Breath of Fire can be of great help because it cleans out the lungs.

SEGMENTED BREATHING

Segmented Breathing entails the use of a specific ratio of breaths. For instance, a technique might require you to inhale in four parts and exhale in four parts. More about Segmented Breathing in subsequent chapters.

MUDRAS

Mudras are hand or body positions which are maintained during an exercise or meditation. These positions make important connections in the nervous system and stimulate specific energy pathways. In addition, Mudras are said to increase circulation to different areas of the brain and/or important nerve junctures and glands.

When we meditate in Kundalini Yoga, unless otherwise specified, our hands are in Gyan (Wisdom) Mudra. To assume Gyan Mudra, connect the tips of your thumbs and index fingers. The other fingers remain straight.

FOCUS OF THE EYES

Unless otherwise specified, we keep our eyes closed during the exercises. This helps us to recycle energy we'd otherwise be expending through looking. In addition, as our eyes are closed we have them looking up and in, towards the brow. This point, on a line between the eyebrows about an inch above the bridge of the nose, is called the Third Eye.

The Third Eye is the etheric counterpart of the pituitary gland. Whereas our two eyes give us outer sight, the Third Eye supplies insight. The pituitary is called the Master Gland. When we stimulate the Third Eye, we are in a better position to master ourselves.

It's important to realize that when the eyes are fixed the mind is fixed. If you've ever talked to someone whose eyes are darting all over the place, it's a sure sign they're thinking about something else. As we focus at the Third Eye, we're increasing our capacity for intuition and concentration and are raising the frequency of the energy we're gathering through the technique, so that self-healing and expansion can occur more expeditiously.

If focusing up to the brow continues to be uncomfortable for you, then have your eyes one-tenth open, looking down towards the tip of the nose.

BASIC BODY LOCKS

These are combinations of muscle contractions which help to consolidate and enhance the effects of Kundalini Yoga exercises and meditations. They are Root Lock, Diaphragm Lock, Neck Lock, and the use of all of them in concert, called Maha Bhand or Great Lock. Root Lock (Mul Bhand) entails the simultaneous contraction of the anal sphincter and sex organ, while pulling the navel in. Diaphragm Lock is applied by pulling the diaphragm up under the ribs. Unless otherwise specified, use this only when the breath is held out. Neck Lock involves pulling your chin back like a soldier at attention, so that you feel a slight pressure at the back and sides of the neck. Always use Neck Lock while holding the breath in or out, and while meditating. Maha Bhand, as explained, is the contraction of all the locks at once.

Unless otherwise specified, you can apply Mul Bhand at the end of an exercise while holding the breath in and out.

Mantras

Words unlike all others,
Have only one destination: You!

–Odysseus Elytis

In Kundalini Yoga we use certain Words of Power, which, as proud cousins of the First Cause ("In the Beginning was the Word..."), can help you be the successful architect of your existence.

These are called *mantras*. A mantra is a coded sound or phrase with a specific vibratory effect on consciousness. For instance, the word "table" is an abstract representation of a concrete thing. A mantra is considered to be the thing itself.

Unless otherwise specified, during and between the exercises and relaxations we concentrate on and resonate with an important mantra. It's "Sat Nam" (rhymes with "But Mom"). It's a Universal Sound, meaning True Identity, or the Highest Frequency which you, in essence, embody.

"Sat Nam" is a Bij (seed) mantra. From the very first time you say or think it, you plant a seed in your center which gestates and blossoms over time, especially as you water it with your practice. It is the process of becoming more yourself.

As we practice Kundalini Yoga, we think "Sat" on the inhale, "Nam" on the exhale. We intone these to the rhythm and length of the breath being used.

There are a many important reasons for working on the mind as we work on the body. First of all, our minds are like broken records, constantly replaying the patterns of the past. We want our lives choreographed to the impulsations of a deeper sway.

Secondly, Kundalini Yoga is based on the proposition that if we can do something in one hour instead of five hours, with no more effort expended, why not? By meditating on "Sat Nam" along with the exercises, we expand the scope of the technique and contract for a more lucrative payback on our time and effort.

As we inhale "Sat" and exhale "Nam" during or between an exercise, we're not only clearing your mind of deep-seated stress, and making the technique far more effective, but in relating to our Higher Selves with every breath, we're speeding up our personal growth immeasurably. Our minds are hungry for this type of vibration, the way a dry sponge is starved for water.

See Appendix 3 for a list of the major mantras in Kundalini Yoga.

MEDITATION

Ultimately, a state of meditation means to become one with the object of one's focus. The process of meditation is somewhat less glamorous. It entails clearing out the attic of your subconscious mind so that the ceiling of your psyche doesn't cave in on your life. Thoughts will come as you meditate. As soon as you're aware of this, bring your mind back to the mantra and/or task at hand.

You may find yourself having thoughts which relate to current problems or concerns as you meditate. Very often this is deep-seated stress taking the form of topical tension, in much the same way as a rusting car dredged from a pond is brought up covered with the algae and dead leaves which had been floating on the surface.

It's also possible, to varying degrees, to experience some seemingly dramatic phenomena while meditating. Actually, the likelihood of this is usually directly proportionate to the amount of mental and physical purification one needs. For instance, someone who's had a history of drug use will probably have many things come up as the Yoga and Meditation clear mental and physical impurities. Consider this story:

> A group of Buddhist monks were doing their morning meditation. All of a sudden, a young monk saw the Heavens, the Buddhas, Patriarchs, and Divine Beings inhabiting many Paradises, each more beautiful than the last. He cried out to the Head Abbott, "Master, Master, I'm having this incredible vision of the Buddhas and Heavenly Realms! What should I do?" "Keep meditating," the Abbott replied. "It'll go away."

We all have a longing for the miraculous, and at some point you may in fact have an experience beyond the ken of reason. Have no expectations while meditating. Don't get caught up in trying to interpret every sensation and off-the-wall thought or image you perceive. True Spiritual Experience needs no interpretation. Very often it's a heartfelt certainty of the right course to take.

KEEPING UP

There's a saying, "It takes money to make money." In much the same way, it takes spirit to activate Spirit (Kundalini). When you get to a point in each exercise where you feel you can't go on, reexamine that impulse. Always proceed with prudence, but never forget that when you're aspiring to your Infinite aspect, your body and mind have the innate capacity to support you, and will if you so command them to. When you make keeping up a habit, life's tests are no longer curses, but confirmations of Consciousness.

In Kundalini Yoga we not only want to exercise fortitude, but exactitude as well. Kundalini Yoga is the science of angles, triangles, and how energy directed along certain lines becomes exponential. Accordingly, it's important that you strive to perfect the poses to the best of your ability.

In your quest to keep up, learn to tell the difference between discomfort and pain. Discomfort can be a great Teacher, but if you feel you're running a risk of hurting yourself by doing an exercise as given, simply modify the exercise to your capability. Modifications for many of the exercises in this book are given as part of the explanatory text accompanying the sets. The bottom line is, do what you can as best you can, and remember:

IF YOU KEEP UP, YOU'LL BE KEPT UP; YOUR SPIRIT WILL
ALWAYS BE AVAILABLE TO YOU, AND GREATNESS WILL BECOME A CONSTANT
IN EVERYTHING YOU DO AND ARE.

TIME OF THE EXERCISES

Within the time frame specified for an exercise, certain physiological shifts occur which further the process we're trying to achieve. During an exercise, these shifts may be marked by some resistance or negativity on your part. And then the real exercise begins. Keep up! If you're a beginner in this type of work, you can gradually build up to the times as given.

THE SCIENCE OF SEQUENCE

The most sophisticated computer program, a chess match, and, for that matter, every calculated human endeavor, are all predicated on one factor: What happens next, and how will it, modify, reflect on, or enhance, what came before in relation to what will be?

Kundalini Yoga sets are not just random groups of exercises. Each set in Kundalini Yoga addresses many levels at once, and has been formulated in recognition of the working relationship among the various systems that comprise us.

Kundalini Yoga sets engender a synergistic effect, greater than the sum of the parts. Any exercise or group of exercises that fulfills this requirement is called a Kriya. Translated, this means completed action.

Of course you can feel free to practice any exercise in this book by itself. Just one exercise can make a difference in your day. But, time permitting, for the most powerful effects, practice the sets as given.

EASY POSE

Easy Pose is a basic cross-legged position. While meditating between exercises, the wrists are on the knees, palms facing slightly up, elbows ideally straight, index fingers and thumbtips meeting. If a cross-legged position is uncomfortable for you, sit on a pillow, against a wall, or in a chair. Keep your spine straight and hips square.

RELAXATION

The ability to relax is a great and graceful art. For all too many it is a lost art. In Kundalini Yoga we relax on our backs at intervals during every sequence. This allows the benefits of the exercises to be integrated and consolidated in us.

As we lie on our backs, the palms face up. The feet are comfortably apart. Unless a sequence indicates that you move on immediately, feel free to relax on your back after any exercise or group of exercises.

TUNING IN TO BEGIN

Traditionally, most systems of prayer, meditation, and spiritual exercise begin with an invocation, to a Higher Power, god, or patron. This is done out of reverence and with an attitude of gratitude.

In Kundalini Yoga we invoke our Higher Self, within and without, to give us the energy and impetus to keep up. We also open ourselves to guidance for protection and inspiration. To accomplish this we chant the following mantra three times to begin each class or practice session. The mantra is:

This means:

INFINITE CREATIVE CONSCIOUSNESS, I CALL ON YOU.
DIVINE WISDOM WITHIN, I CALL ON YOU.

If you are not in a position to do this out loud, at least say it to yourself. This mantra is a very important part of Kundalini Yoga and should not be overlooked.

GENERAL GUIDELINES

- ❖ It's best not to have eaten two to three hours before practicing yoga.

- ❖ When at all possible, do yoga in clean and accommodating environments.

- ❖ Wear clothes you can comfortably move in (natural fibers are best).

- ❖ It's best to do yoga barefoot.

- ❖ Keep your spine and shoulders covered (with a shawl, blanket, or sweater, etc.) while doing any extended meditation.

- ❖ Never practice yoga under the influence of drugs or alcohol. If you're taking medication under the supervision of a physician, consult him/her before proceeding.

- ❖ Don't aggravate an existing injury. If you're creative, you can work around it and ultimately help the healing process.

- ❖ Pregnant women should consult their physicians before proceeding. Generally, extra caution should be exercised after the fourth month. Contact a Kundalini Yoga Teacher for guidelines.

- ❖ When a woman is menstruating, she should substitute Long Deep Breathing for Breath of Fire and choose sets of moderate difficulty.

- ❖ Try to set aside a time each day to do your practice.

TO REITERATE...

So, you're almost ready to roll up your sleeves and get down to business. Here's a recapitulation of the basics:

**BEGIN EACH SESSION BY CHANTING
ONG NAMO GURU DEV NAMO THREE TIMES.**

AND UNLESS OTHERWISE SPECIFIED:

1. All breathing is done through the nose.

2. Your eyes are closed and turned up towards the brow.

3. Throughout each session, during and between the exercises, inhale think "Sat" and exhale think "Nam." As soon as you notice your mind wandering, bring it back.

4. While meditating between exercises, the wrists are on the knees with the palms facing slightly up. The hands are in Gyan Mudra, index fingers and thumbtips meeting.

5. In the context of a sequence relax on your back, at the very least, after every two or three exercises.

6. Wrap your arms around your bent knees, tuck your nose between the knees, and rock back and forth on your spine a few times after relaxing on your back.

7. At the end of each exercise inhale, hold the breath, and apply Mul Bhand (squeeze up on the anal sphincter and sex organ as you pull the navel in), then exhale, hold the breath out, and apply Mul Bhand. Do this one to three times.

8. While holding the breath in or out, and while meditating, apply Neck Lock. This entails pulling your chin back like a soldier at attention so that you feel a slight pressure at the back and sides of the neck.

MIX & MATCH

What follows in Chapters 4–6 are six groups (A through F), each divided into four sequences. Each sequence is comprised of three exercises, making a total of 72 exercises. To design a session, you can do one or more of the sequences from each of the groups A–F. Practice the sequences in the order given for each group and finish up with a Meditation from Chapter 13 and/or 14 and/or by chanting a Mantra you're familiar with from Appendix 3.

One or more of the sequences from groups A through C will also serve as an effective warm-up for the Meditations in Chapter 13 and/or 14 (as well as other Meditations in this book), and/or the chanting of any Mantra you're familiar with from Appendix 3.

In addition, one of more of the sequences from groups A through C will fulfill daily maintenance requirements and round out longer sets in Chapters 7 through 11.

Please refer to Page 152 for an pictorial overview of the above formula for creating your own warm-up sets. (It's not as hard as it sounds!)

GO!
YOU'VE READ THIS FAR. YOU CAN EITHER LET THIS BOOK COLLECT DUST OR USE IT AS AN ENCYCLOPEDIA OF SPIRIT AND GAIN THE ENERGY AND AWARENESS TO BE THE ANSWER TO YOUR OWN PRAYERS. TURN THIS PAGE AND TURN A FATE INTO A DESTINY!

CHAPTER 4

WARM-UPS FOR FLEXIBILITY & FOUNDATION

GROUP A

SEQUENCE 1

EXERCISE 1

Sit cross-legged. Press your hands together (Prayer Pose) with the thumbs against the sternum (FIGURE 1). As you inhale, raise your right arm to 60 degrees as both knees rise up. Exhale and clap your hands as they come back into Prayer Pose on the exhale. Now, inhale, raising your left arm to 60 degrees as both knees come up. Exhale down and clap (FIGURE 2). Continue 1–3 minutes.

MODIFICATION: If you tilt back when you raise your knees, sit on a pillow.

FIGURE 1   FIGURE 2

This exercise creates a line of stretch into the sacral area of the lower back. It also works on brain hemisphere balancing, the heart, Heart Center, immune system, and lymphatic system.

EXERCISE 2

Sit cross-legged. Have your fingertips in front of you on the floor. Flex your spine. Inhale as you press your lower spine forward (FIGURE 3). Exhale as you flex it back (FIGURE 4). Continue at a good pace. 1–3 minutes.

MODIFICATION: Hold onto your shins or knees or sit in a chair.

The flexion movement of the lower spine in conjunction with the breathing engenders flexibility and insulates one against injury. In addition, by stimulating the area of the fourth vertebra energy is released and directed towards the process of self-healing and self-expansion.

FIGURE 3

FIGURE 4

FIGURE 5

EXERCISE 3

Washing Machine. Your hands are on your shoulders, fingers in front, thumbs in back. As you inhale twist left, and as you exhale twist right (FIGURE 5). It's a continuous movement. Turn your head with your body. 1–3 minutes.

This is a complementary movement to the previous exercise. It helps to open up the lungs and midriff area and keeps the rib cage from getting rigid.

> **BOW TO THREE THINGS:**
> **TRUTH,**
> **YOUR HIGHER SELF,**
> **AND GOD.**
> –*Yogi Bhajan*

EXERCISE 1

Sit crosslegged. Hold onto your knees and grind your stomach in a circumference described by the outside of the knees (FIGURE 1). Don't lean forward; move the midriff. You're not compressing the lower back, you're elongating it. Create a heat in the lower spine. Go 26 rotations in each direction.

Exercise 1 adjusts the ileocecal valve, tonifies the inner organs, increases peristaltic motion in the intestines, stimulates the fire energy at the navel, and prepares the lower back for more exercises.

FIGURE 1

FIGURE 2

EXERCISE 2

Drop your head forward and slowly roll your head around in a big slow careful circle (FIGURE 2). Follow the course of the collarbone. Don't gloss over areas of tension, rather work through them. Roll your head 11 times one way and 11 times the other. Take at least eight seconds per complete turn.

MODIFICATION: If you don't feel it's prudent to drop your head all the way back, simply draw a circle in the air with your nose.

Exercise 2 seems simplistic but offers a wide range of benefits. It prepares small vertebrae in the neck for the next exercise and alleviates neck and shoulder tension so that circulation flows unimpeded upwards. Our brains require 60% of the oxygen we breathe; thus, this exercise literally constitutes food for thought! Neck rolls help the thyroid and parathyroid glands and stimulate the Throat Center, the seat of communication and creativity. This exercise also works the meridians running through the neck, improves short-term memory and eyesight, and can help open blocked sinuses.

EXERCISE 3

This is called Cat/Cow and is done on the hands and knees. As you inhale press your head up and stomach towards the ground. This is Cow Pose (FIGURE 3). As you exhale drop your head and curve your spine. This is Cat Pose (FIGURE 4). Move at a moderate to fast pace for 1 to 3 minutes.

VISUALIZATION: As you exhale into Cat Pose, imagine a whip cracking up your spine, the tip of which flicks the top of your head from the inside of your skull.

FIGURE 3

FIGURE 4

Cat/Cow stimulates and aligns the entire spine, all 26 vertebrae. Given that the spine is the conduit for the central nervous system, Cat/Cow can be said to work on all 72,000 nerves. It also stimulates the optic nerve to give you sparkling eyes, and engenders emotional balance.

SEQUENCE 3

EXERCISE 1

Sit on your heels. Extend your right leg straight back. Have your left foot flat, left knee bent, and lunge forward. The fingertips are framing the left foot. Look up and stare at a point on the ceiling (FIGURE 1). Long Deep Breathing. 1–3 minutes. Switch sides and repeat. Relax on your back before continuing.

FIGURE 1

This exercise stretches the quadricep muscles on top of the thighs as a complement to subsequent stretching. It also works on the liver and stomach meridians and loosens up the hips. Staring upwards helps balance the sympathetic and parasympathetic nervous systems.

EXERCISE 2

Lie on your back with your feet flat on the floor, knees bent. Press your hips up and interlace your fingers under you. Get your shoulders under you too (FIGURE 2). Breath of Fire. 1–3 minutes.

FIGURE 2

This is a counterpose to the next exercise. It helps the liver's function of purifying the blood. This exercise also opens up circulation to the extremities.

Exercise 3

Have your legs in front of you, feet flexed. Your arms are parallel to the ground, fingers straight, thumbs up. As you inhale lean back 30 degrees (Figure 3), and as you exhale go forward 30 degrees (Figure 4). Continue at a moderate pace with a deep breath. 1–3 minutes.

Figure 3

Figure 4

This exercise works on the adrenals, kidneys, lungs, and sciatic nerve.
In addition, it helps to open the solar plexus to prepare you for subsequent stretching.

> OUR NERVES ARE A FIELD OF FLOWERS
> ONLY YOU CAN WALK ON;
> YOU ARE THE LIGHT OF THE BREATH
> A GENTLE WIND FROM HEAVEN.

EXERCISE 1

This one's called Frog Pose. Start on your toes in a squatting position. Your heels are together and your feet are apart. Your knees are wide. Your arms are inside your knees. You're on your fingertips (FIGURE 1). The elbows stay straight throughout the whole exercise. As you inhale, straighten your knees and lower your head (FIGURE 2). As you exhale, return to the original position. Do this 26, 54, or 108 times.

MODIFICATION: To straighten the legs, let go of the ground on the inhale.

Frog Pose stimulates cardiovascular capability, strengthens the nerves to make you a more potent person, and shapes and strengthens the legs.

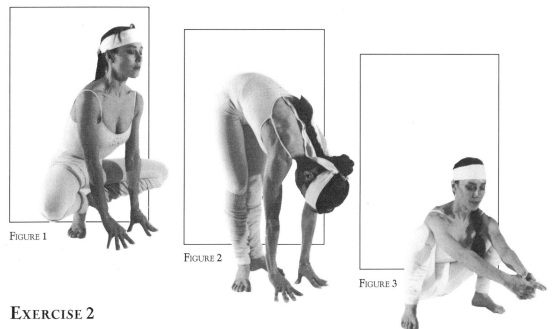

FIGURE 1

FIGURE 2

FIGURE 3

EXERCISE 2

Crow Pose. Assume a squatting position, ideally with your feet flat and toes pointing forward. The arms are straight and rest on the knees (FIGURE 3). Breath of Fire. 1–2 minutes.

MODIFICATION: If keeping the feet flat is too difficult, be on your toes.

Crow Pose is a complementary pose to the next exercise. It also realigns the colon and helps to "ground" a person by working on the earth element associated with the first center of consciousness corresponding to the rectum.

EXERCISE 3

Have your legs in front of you. Raise the left leg and hold the left heel with the left hand and pull back on the toes with the right hand (FIGURE 4). Try to sit up straight. Breath of Fire. 1–3 minutes. Switch sides and repeat.

MODIFICATION: If necessary, hold under your ankle, calf, or knee.

FIGURE 4

This pose stretches the sciatic nerve. This is the longest nerve in the nervous system and has a tie-in with every system in the body. In Kundalini Yoga we call this the life nerve. It's said that if you can keep this nerve flexible, you can literally lengthen your life. Stretching the life nerve also stimulates the bladder meridian which runs up the back of the leg. This engenders emotional balance (by adjusting the water element in you). Do this or a similar exercise every day. Remember this maxim: When your life nerve is tight, something's not right.

> RELAX AND FEEL DESERVING
> OF THE BOUNTY OF THE BREATH
> AND THE GIFTS OF GRACE
> YOU'VE CONTRACTED FOR
> RELAX TO YOUR VERY INNER CORE
> RELAX MORE.

GROUP B
SEQUENCE 1

EXERCISE 1

Tree Pose. Standing. Place the top of the right foot on the left thigh. Lean over and support yourself with your hands (FIGURE 1). Long Deep Breathing. 3–5 minutes. Repeat with the other leg.

MODIFICATION: Cross the right leg in front of the left. The right knee will be bent with the toes of the right foot on the floor to the left side of the left leg. The left leg remains straight. If you can't get your hands to the ground, simply hang over.

Tree Pose works on the sciatic nerve and strengthens the legs so you won't have to rely on a cane, walker, wheelchair, or golf cart for mobility when you're older. It helps prevent varicose veins and builds your nervous system so you can weather the tests of the times with ease.

FIGURE 1

FIGURE 2

EXERCISE 2

Archer Pose. Standing: your feet shoulder-width apart, toes pointing forward. Turn the right foot 90 degrees to the right. Press the left heel three inches to the outside. Bend the right knee, in line with the right foot. The left hand is behind the left ear in a fist, the right arm straight, also a fist. Stretch across the sternum. Stare straight out over the right hand. Long Deep Breathing. 3–5 minutes. Switch sides and repeat (FIGURE 2).

Archer Pose also works on the entire nervous system. It puts you under pressure to release the deeper pressure a lifetime of stress has imposed. It stimulates the area on the inner thigh just above the knee, a very important point in the nervous system related to the assimilation of calcium via the thigh bone.

EXERCISE 3

Sit between your heels. Lie back and interlace your fingers over your navel. Breath of Fire (FIGURE 3). 1–3 minutes.

MODIFICATION: Lie on your back with the soles of the feet together and knees bent. Interlace your fingers over your navel.

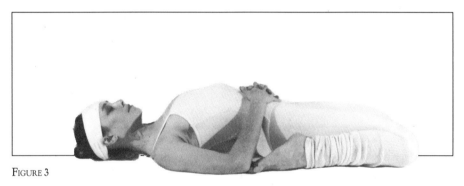

FIGURE 3

This pose releases tension in the lower nerve plexi which translates into blocks around sexuality and basic security or survival. In conjunction with the previous two exercises, it revitalizes the nervous system and makes energy available for meditation.

YOU DID IT
NOW LET IT BE DONE FOR YOU
RELAX THROUGH AND THROUGH
UNTO THE ALL IN ALL
LET YOUR BODY FALL
SPIRIT RISE.

SEQUENCE 2

❖◆❖

EXERCISE 1

Have the soles of the feet together. Pull your feet towards you. Hold onto your feet. Angle forward. Use your elbows as levers against the inside portion of the calves or front of the shins. Feel a radical stretch on the inner thighs. Long Deep Breathing (FIGURE 1). 1–3 minutes.

This works the sex nerve, which runs along the inside of the thigh. If the sex nerve is chronically tight, a person tends to be either obsessed with sex and its cultural accoutrements or too puritanical about it. As in everything, Kundalini Yoga advocates balance. This pose also stimulates the kidney meridian.

EXERCISE 2

Extend your legs in front of you. Support yourself with your hands. Point the toes. The feet are off the ground throughout. Inhale as you straighten the legs (FIGURE 2). Exhale as the legs go wide (FIGURE 3), inhale as you bring them together (FIGURE 2). Exhale as you bend your knees into your body (FIGURE 4). Continue rhythmically. The movement can be described by the words: out, apart, together, in. 1½ minutes.

MODIFICATION: Keep your legs on the floor throughout the exercise.

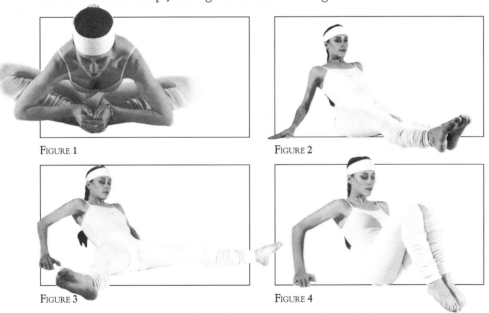

FIGURE 1   FIGURE 2

FIGURE 3   FIGURE 4

Exercise 2 serves as a segue from the previous exercise. It works the sex nerve as well as the spleen and kidney meridians. The movement enhances this sequence's ability to transmute energy from the lower to the higher centers for the purpose of self-healing and self-expansion.

EXERCISE 3

Kundalini Lotus Pose. Wrap the first two fingers of either hand around the corresponding big toes. Balance on the sacrum. Extend your legs up and out (FIGURE 5). Breath of Fire. 1–3 minutes.

MODIFICATION: Hold under your knees or support yourself with your hands behind you. For more of a challenge, hold your heels or insteps. If you have trouble keeping your balance, open your eyes and anchor yourself by staring at something.

FIGURE 5

Kundalini Lotus Pose transmutes sexual and digestive energies
to the brain and higher centers. It also engenders mental and physical balance.

YOUR RIVERS OF LIGHT
COURSE THROUGH ME;
I CURE MY THIRST
REPEATING THEIR NAMES.

EXERCISE 1

Chair Pose. Standing. With your back to a wall, slide down, thighs are parallel and forelegs perpendicular to the floor (FIGURE 1). Breath of Fire. 1–3 minutes.

VARIATION: Standing. The feet are shoulder-width apart, slightly angled out. Your back is like a tabletop relative to the floor. Your hands go inside the legs and grab your ankles.

Chair Pose strengthens the nervous system and will make you a more potent person.
It also works on muscle groups which complement the next exercise.

FIGURE 1

FIGURE 2

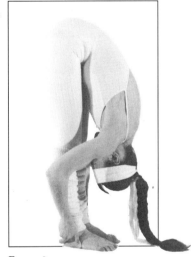

FIGURE 3

EXERCISE 2

Standing. Lean over and hold under the toes. As you inhale, stretch up (FIGURE 2). As you exhale, grab behind your ankles and pull your nose towards your knees (FIGURE 3). Continue slowly for 1–3 minutes.

This exercise stretches the sciatic nerve and helps to open the solar plexus,
a prerequisite for safe and successful stretching.

EXERCISE 3

Be on your hands and knees. As you inhale, swing your left leg up and raise your head (FIGURE 4). As you exhale, the knee comes up and head goes down (FIGURE 5). 1–3 minutes. Switch sides and repeat.

FIGURE 4

FIGURE 5

This exercise adjusts the navel point and balances prana and apana (Expanding and Eliminating energies), which blend and balance at the solar plexus. According to Yoga it's essential for these energies to be balanced for one to be healthy.

THE PORTFOLIO OF THE PURE ONE HAS DIVERSIFIED
WITH STOCK IN EVERY SOUL
AND NO ONE HAS DENIED THE BEAUTY THEY SEEK.

SEQUENCE 4

◆◇◆

EXERCISE 1

Frog Pose. Start on your toes in a squatting position. Your heels are together and your feet are apart. Your knees are wide. Your arms are inside your knees. You're on your fingertips (FIGURE 1). The elbows stay straight throughout the whole exercise. As you inhale, straighten your knees and lower your head (FIGURE 2). As you exhale, return to the original position. Do this at a good pace 26, 54, or 108 times.

FIGURE 1   FIGURE 2

EXERCISE 2

Camel Pose. Start in a kneeling position. Reach back and hold your ankles or heels. Your head drops back (FIGURE 3). Breath of Fire. 1–3 minutes. NOTE: Upon inhaling, open your eyes to prevent light-headedness. Come out of the pose very slowly.

MODIFICATION: Kneel and interlace your fingers behind your back.

FIGURE 3

Camel Pose releases blocks in the lower centers which manifest as low self-esteem or sense of self at odds with reality. It also stimulates the digestive meridians. Thus, Camel Pose can be very useful in overcoming food and substance addictions and is excellent for women, as it prevents tension around the ovaries and stimulates the lymphatic system as a measure against breast cancer. For men, it builds the sexual nervous system and releases armoring in the chest area, expressed as hard-heartedness and a lack of compassion.

EXERCISE 3

Sat Kriya. Sit on your heels. Raise your arms up so that the upper arms are hugging the ears. Interlace your fingers with the index fingers extended, thumbs crossed (FIGURE 4). As you say "Sat," pull the navel in towards the spine. As you say "Nam," relax the navel. The breath will take care of itself. Be sure to keep the elbows straight throughout the exercise. 3 minutes.

VISUALIZATION: As you say "Sat," feel the sound explode in the navel. As you say "Nam," feel the sound rising up the spine and imagine it bursting like a supernova in the center of the brain.

FIGURE 4

Sat Kriya is one of the basic exercises in Kundalini Yoga. It's a powerful therapy for overcoming deep insecurities, fears, and personality disorders. Sat Kriya directly stimulates the Kundalini process. With sensible practice, you can build up the time of practice to 11 and, ultimately, 31 minutes.

NOTE: ALWAYS RELAX AFTER PRACTICING SAT KRIYA FOR A TIME EQUAL TO THE LENGTH OF THE EXERCISE.

CHAPTER 5

THE SEAT OF POWER
GROUP C

The following exercises work on developing the Navel Center, an etheric vortex of energy related to will, focus, and the ability to be unexploitable and undefeatable.

The Navel Center is the most important of the Chakras. You may own the most powerful state-of-the-art computer, but if you have nowhere to plug it in, it won't do you any good. The Navel Center supplies energy to the other centers which comprise your totality. It must be consolidated and strengthened before higher mental states become a practical reality in one's life. This center relates to the element fire. It literally gives you energy to burn. When activated, it sheds light on your fears as the rising sun exposes the gnarled tree trunk campers were convinced was a monster!

The Navel Center is called the *Manipura Chakra*, which means "many jewels." Our power and potentialities are buried here as uncut gems, waiting to be faceted, polished, and set in a crown.

Also, in the manner of fire, the Navel Center, when well developed, helps absorb and purify obstacles in life. As Britain once ruled the world on the strength of its Navy, so, too, can you rule your world through Navel power!

The following exercises will also tone and strengthen the abdominal area and improve digestive system functioning.

NOTE: BE SURE YOU'RE PROPERLY WARMED UP BEFORE PROCEEDING WITH THE FOLLOWING EXERCISES.

SEQUENCE 1

EXERCISE 1

Wheel Pose. Lie on your back with your feet flat and knees bent. Your hands are under the shoulders, palms down, fingers pointing back towards the feet. Straighten your arms so that your back and head come off the floor and the navel above the knees (FIGURE 1). Breath of Fire. 1 minute.

MODIFICATION: I call this Training Wheel Pose. Lie on your back with your feet flat and knees bent. Press your hips up and interlace your fingers under you. Tuck your shoulders under you, too.

FIGURE 1

Wheel Pose elongates the abdominal muscles as a prelude and enhancement to abdominal strengthening. It centers the Navel Point, brings flexibility to the spine, and helps the digestive system.

IN THE MOMENT
WE ARE ABOUT
TO BE IN
YOU ARE WAITING,
COUNTING SNOWFLAKES
ON YOUR ABACUS OF ALWAYS.

EXERCISE 2

Stretch Pose. Lie on your back. Your hands are under the buttocks, palms down. Raise your head and heels 6 inches. Stare at your toes. The toes are pointed (FIGURE 2). Breath of Fire. 1–3 minutes.

MODIFICATION: Do one leg at a time. Hold each one up for equal duration.

FIGURE 2

Stretch Pose strengthens and adjusts the Navel Point and strengthens the abdominal muscles. Having the eyes open, staring at the toes, works on the sympathetic nervous system. Having the toes pointed stimulates circulation.

EXERCISE 3

Parallel Bicycle. Lie on your back, hands under the buttocks, palms down. Extend your legs so that the heels are 1½ feet off the ground. As you inhale, bring your left knee into the body and, as you exhale, bring your right knee in as the left leg extends. 1–2 minutes. This is actually more of a piston-like motion rather than a bicycling movement. Feel yourself funnelling energy in through the navel. Breathe powerfully (FIGURE 3).

MODIFICATION: Keep your knees somewhat bent throughout the exercise.

FIGURE 3

SEQUENCE 2

EXERCISE 1

Lie on your back (FIGURE 1). Inhale. As you exhale, swing your legs over, to, or towards the floor behind you. Move with control (FIGURE 2). Continue 1–3 minutes inhaling down, exhaling as you move the legs towards the floor behind you.

MODIFICATION: If you can't get your feet to the floor behind you, go half way. If this is too difficult, bring your bent knees in towards the body on the exhale.

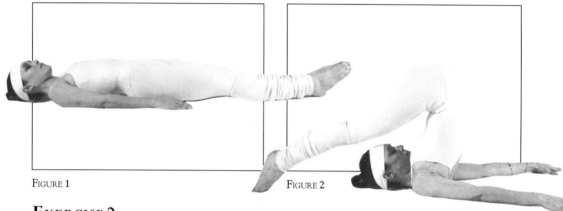

FIGURE 1   FIGURE 2

EXERCISE 2

Lie on your back (FIGURE 3). Inhale. Exhale, sit up, hold onto your feet or ankles, and briefly pull your nose towards your knees. Continue for 1–3 minutes.

MODIFICATION: Bend your knees and/or use your hands to help you sit up.

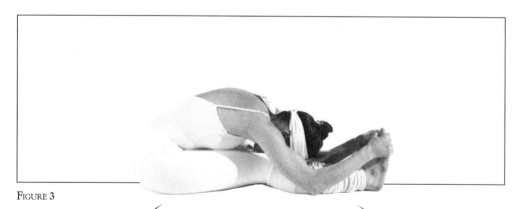

FIGURE 3

PUT YOUR BODY ON THE LINE
AS A FORM OF PRAISE.

EXERCISE 3

Lie on your back (FIGURE 4). Inhale. Exhale as you swing your legs over into Plow Pose (FIGURE 5). Inhale as you lie down again (FIGURE 4). Exhale as you sit up, hold onto your feet or ankles, and briefly pull your nose towards the knees (FIGURE 6). 1–3 minutes.

MODIFICATION: Refer to the modifications for the previous two exercises.

FIGURE 4

FIGURE 5

FIGURE 6

SEQUENCE 3

EXERCISE 1

Lie on your stomach. Bend your knees and flex your feet. Hold onto your ankles and arch up into Bow Pose (FIGURE 1). Rock on your stomach. Inhale back and exhale forward. Do this 26 times.

MODIFICATION: To modify this, try the following: Simply hold Bow Pose with Long Deep Breathing or interlace your fingers behind your back, pull your arms off the back, cross your ankles as the knees are bent, and gently rock on the stomach.

FIGURE 1

Exercise 1 is extremely beneficial for the digestive system. It also tonifies and flushes the internal organs and can help keep you young. You can increase the amount of time you do this with practice.

FIGURE 2

EXERCISE 2

Stretch Pose. Lie on your back, hands under the buttocks, palms down. Raise your head and heels 6 inches. Stare at your toes (FIGURE 2). Breath of Fire. 1–3 minutes.

MODIFICATION: Raise one leg at a time.

EXERCISE 3

Lie on your back. Your arms are above you on the floor (FIGURE 3). Inhale. Exhale as you raise your right arm and left leg straight up (FIGURE 4). Inhale as you lower the arm and leg. Exhale raise the other two. Continue these alternate leg and arms lifts to and from 90 degrees. 3 minutes.

MODIFICATION: If your lower back feels put-upon, keep your knees bent throughout this exercise.

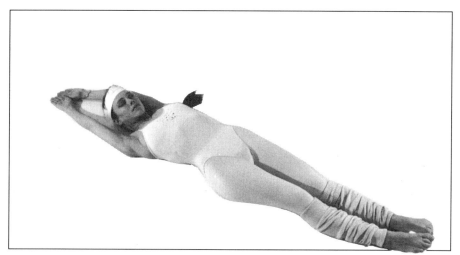

FIGURE 3

FIGURE 4

This exercise puts the Navel Point in proper alignment and balances the brain hemispheres as well.

Sequence 4

Exercise 1

Lie on your stomach. Your hands are under the shoulders, palms facing down. Inhale as you raise your upper body (Figure 1). Exhale as you come down. Keep your hips on the ground, your lower back relaxed. As you come up press your shoulders down and head back to follow the curve of the spine. Do this 26 times.

Modification: Move your hands further forward and/or don't come up as high.

Figure 1

Cobra Pose flushes out the kidneys, fosters flexibility of the spine, and elongates the abdominal muscles in preparation for the leg lift-type exercise to follow.

Exercise 2

Lie on your stomach. Your hands are in fists with the thumbs inside the fists. Place this configuration under the hips where the thighs meet the body. Cross your ankles. Lift your legs and upper body (Figure 2). Breath of Fire. 1–3 minutes.

Modification: Bend your knees and/or raise one leg at a time.

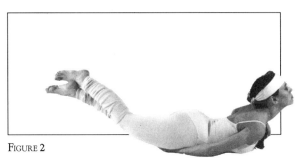

Figure 2

This exercise revitalizes the adrenals and strengthens the lower back and hip adductor muscles. For women, it helps to neutralize tension in the ovary area. This exercise also elongates the abdominal muscles in preparation for the next exercise.

EXERCISE 3

Lie on your back. Your hands are under the buttocks, palms facing down. As you inhale, raise both legs straight up to 90 degrees (FIGURE 3). Exhale as you lower them. Do this 26 to 54 times. NOTE: If your lower back feels put-upon, feel free to use the modification suggested below.

MODIFICATION: Keep your knees bent throughout the exercise.

FIGURE 3

*Double leg lifts strengthen the Navel Point and correct
the upper digestive system. This exercise also works on the heart and lungs.*

BE REELED IN
BY THE GOLDEN CORD
CAST BY THE ANGLER
OF ALL THAT IS.

IN THE DESERT OF THE HEART
LET THE HEALING FOUNTAIN START.
IN THE PRISON OF HIS DAYS
TEACH THE FREE MAN HOW TO PRAISE.
                                    –W.H. Auden

CHAPTER 6

HEART & SOUL

GROUP D
SEQUENCE 1

EXERCISE 1

Sit on your heels. Your hands are on the thighs. The palms face down. As you inhale, flex your lower spine forward (FIGURE 1). Exhale as you flex back (FIGURE 2). 1–3 minutes.

MODIFICATION: If you can't sit on your heels, cross your legs and grab your knees.

FIGURE 1

FIGURE 2

This exercise helps to open the solar plexus which is intrinsic to flexibility, energy in-flow, and emotional and energy balance. It is also good for the liver.

Exercise 2

Assume a front push-up position. The toes are not curled under. Your head is up and your eyes are open, staring straight ahead (Figure 3). Breathe long and deeply for 45 seconds, then do Breath of Fire for 45 seconds.

Modification: If your lower back feels put upon, be on your hands and knees with your feet off the ground.

Figure 3

Exercise 2 helps to open the solar plexus and also strengthens the nerves.

> Each of us
> Has a Destiny to fulfill
> Under the beautiful banner
> Of that will
> Which exists in accordance
> With our excellence
> And inner aims.

EXERCISE 3

Your hands are in Prayer Pose, pressed together, thumbs against the sternum (FIGURE 4). Inhale as you straighten your arms with the palms facing forward and fingers pointing up (FIGURE 5). Exhale as you press the arms straight out to the sides (FIGURE 6). Inhale as you extend the arms in front of you (FIGURE 5). Exhale as you bring your hands into Prayer Pose again (FIGURE 4). The movement can be described by the words: out, apart, together, in. 3–11 minutes.

FIGURE 4

FIGURE 5

FIGURE 6

Exercise 3 works on the Heart Center, immune system, lymphatic system, and brain hemisphere balancing.

SEQUENCE 2

EXERCISE 1

The Propeller Exercise. Sit cross-legged with your left hand at sternum level, palm facing out. Your right hand faces inward. Hook your fingers with the forearms parallel to the floor (FIGURE 1). As you inhale, the left elbow comes up as the right goes down. As you exhale, the right elbow goes up as the left goes down. It's a seesaw motion. Do this with powerful breathing for 3 minutes.

To end, inhale, hold the breath, and try to pull the hands apart. The forearms are parallel. Exhale, hold the breath out, and pull. Be sure your neck is in Neck Lock as the breath is held and expelled. You may repeat this twice more.

The Propeller Exercise strengthens the physical heart, and opens the Heart Center. When you feel like stopping, keep going! Your immune system will "kick in."

FIGURE 1   FIGURE 2   FIGURE 3

EXERCISE 2

Sit cross-legged. Your arms are in front of you at a 45 degree angle, about 10 degrees outside the shoulders. Your palms face up throughout this exercise. Slump back as you say "A," as in father (FIGURE 2). Thrust your sternum forward and make your hands into fists as you say "Hum." Emphasize the "mmm" sound (FIGURE 3). Do this no more than 12 times and always relax on your back afterwards.

Exercise 2 directly stimulates the Heart Center. The sound "Hum" means "we" and is contained in the word "human." To be humanly human, we must open our hearts to an awareness that we're all linked. The first step of Higher Consciousness is shifting our perspective from "me" to "we."

EXERCISE 3

Remain on your back. Lovingly bring your left hand to your lips and kiss the center of the palm (FIGURE 4). Repeat with the right hand. Continue alternately kissing your palms for as long as you'd like.

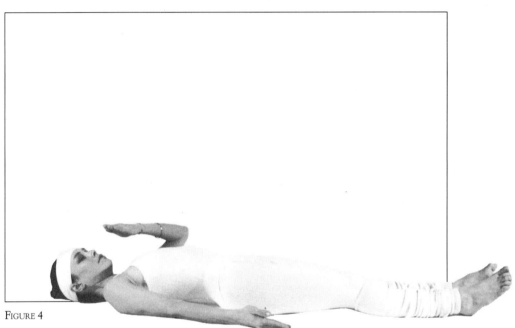

FIGURE 4

This exercise stimulates your capacity for self-nurturing and compassion. The center of the palms is a very important Heart Center point. It also relates to the paracardium, the muscle surrounding the heart. Love begins with loving yourself—not in a narcissistic sense, but with the awareness that you are a creation of the Creator, a sovereign soul, beautiful and blessed.

LET BYGONES BE BYGONES—
FORGIVE AND FORGET;
LIVE TO REMEMBER
THAT YOU ARE YOU
AND THAT FOREVER.

SEQUENCE 3

EXERCISE 1

Your hands are in your lap, fingers interlaced (FIGURE 1). Begin chanting:

GOD AND ME, ME AND GOD, ARE ONE

Do this in a monotone. Emphasize the first word of each phrase by pulling in the navel. Vibrate the entire phrase at the sternum. 3 minutes.

FIGURE 1

This phrase has been formulated, awkward syntax and all, to maintain its vibrational integrity with the added dimension of its meaning, which circumvents your intellect and gives you an affirmation of Infinity. Don't waste time trying to validate or invalidate the existence of God. If you're willing to believe in your Self, you can be said to believe in God. This exercise will help to heal you by stimulating the immune system via the thymus gland and by giving you a sense of the True You which recognizes no imperfection.

EXERCISE 2

Sit up very straight. Keep your rib cage lifted (FIGURE 2). Inhale. Exhale and hold the breath out while pumping your stomach in and out at a good pace. Hold the breath out for as long as you can–past the point of panic. Inhale, exhale, repeat. 3–5 minutes.

Holding the breath out in a conscious manner is powerful and profound. It promotes self-healing by quickening the proliferation of cells. It allows for cleansing and oxygenation of the bloodstream. Also, when you hold the breath out, you simulate a death experience to the psyche. Accordingly, this kind of exercise will help you overcome your deepest fears. Pumping the stomach helps the heart by easing tension in the diaphragm and is an aid to circulation. In addition, as you hold the breath out you create a vacuum in your "Pranic Body" (see Appendix 2). Upon inhaling, you fill with light. In strengthening the Pranic Body, you compensate for stress by helping the adrenals hold a charge.

FIGURE 2

FIGURE 3

EXERCISE 3

Your left hand is on your back, angling up towards the right shoulder, palm facing out (FIGURE 3). Inhale, then exhale and hold the breath out, squeezing the lower nerve plexi, rectum, sex organ, and navel. Inhale when you must, exhale, and continue for 3–5 minutes.

Exercise 3 strengthens the heart and immune system.

SEQUENCE 4

◦◇◦

EXERCISE 1

Sit cross-legged with your fingers on top of the head, on either side of the midline down the center of the skull. Your thumbs close off the ears. Inhale as you turn left (FIGURE 1). Exhale face center. Inhale as you turn right. Repeat. Keep each movement distinct. Don't let your elbows sag. Feel the stretch in your armpits. 3 minutes.

This exercise stimulates the lymph glands in the arms and chest to promote the elimination of toxins. The fingers on top of the head stimulate meridian points relating to the digestive system and elimination.

FIGURE 1   FIGURE 2

EXERCISE 2

Sit cross-legged. Your thumbs are pressing the mounds at the base of the little fingers. The palms face in towards the body. To the rhythm of the Breath of Fire, raise and lower alternate arms to the sides, to and from a 60 degree angle (FIGURE 2). Be sure you straighten the arms as they extend. Move powerfully! 3–4 minutes.

This exercise works on the Heart Center, magnetic field, immune system, and lymphatic system.

EXERCISE 3

Sit cross-legged with your hands on your knees, elbows straight. The palms of the hands face up throughout the entire exercise. Inhale, raise your arms straight up and back as if throwing something behind you (FIGURE 3). Exhale down. Breathe through the open mouth. The exhale will sound like a lion's roar. 4–5 minutes.

FIGURE 3

This is a powerful exercise to cleanse dead cells and mucus from the lungs. After this exercise you will be in a good position to meditate deeply.

RELAX AND
DO A SLOW DISSOLVE;
MELT AWAY
LIKE AN ICE CUBE
ON A SUMMER'S DAY.
EVAPORATE
UNTO THE MOST GREAT.

GROUP E
SEQUENCE 1

———◆◆———

EXERCISE 1

Lie on your back. Swing your legs up into shoulder stand (FIGURE 1). Support your lower back with your hands. Try to get up onto your shoulders. Press your chin firmly against the collarbone. Ideally, there will be a straight line from the shoulders through the heels. Breathe long and deeply for 1–3 minutes, then do Breath of Fire for the same amount of time. If your lower back, neck, or hips feel put-upon, please use the modification below. Your shoulders and elbows should take all the weight.

MODIFICATION: Your legs can be angled back towards the floor and/or you can use a wall to give support to your legs.

FIGURE 1

Shoulder Stand helps oxygenate the brain. Ten minutes in this pose will refresh you to the same extent as two hours of deep sleep. Shoulder Stand also allows for the realignment of internal organs which get pulled out of place by the constant pressure of gravity. It helps prevent varicose veins. Your kidneys love the benefits Shoulder Stand gives them. Shoulder Stand helps your heart and fires up the digestive fire. In the context of this short sequence, Shoulder Stand stimulates the thyroid and parathyroid glands and their etheric counterpart, the Throat Center.

EXERCISE 2

Tuck Pose. Lie on your back. Wrap your arms around bent knees and tuck your nose between the knees (FIGURE 2). Breath of Fire. 1–3 minutes.

Tuck Pose pressurizes the thyroid and parathyroid glands which relate to metabolism, moods, youth, beauty, and the assimilation of nutrients, notably calcium. If you feel a pressure in the back or sides of the neck, it means the exercise is working for you. Keep up! Embrace the discomfort conscious work on yourself sometimes entails as a means to growth and self-healing.

FIGURE 2

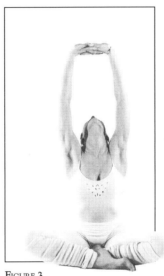

FIGURE 3

EXERCISE 3

Interlace your fingers and raise your arms. Your hands are inverted (FIGURE 3). Drop your head back. Stare at a point on the ceiling. Breath of Fire. 1–3 minutes.

Inhale, hold the breath, and drop your head forward so the chin rests on the collarbone. Rub your head side to side across the collarbone a few times. Keep the arms up, raise your head, facing forward. Focus at the Third Eye. Chant the phrase:

HEALTHY AM I, HAPPY AM I, HOLY AM I

Do this 3–5 times per breath. Continue for up to 5 minutes.

The first and second parts of this exercise draw energy and circulation to the thyroid area and energize the Throat Center. In the last part of the exercise, the sounds "He," "Ha," and "Ho," of Healthy, Happy, and Holy relate to the frequency of the Throat Center. As you utter this affirmation, you're at once empowering yourself to become the living embodiment of this ideal.

SEQUENCE 2

EXERCISE 1

Hold your knees. As you inhale, raise your shoulders up to the ears (FIGURE 1). As you exhale, lower them. Do this with a powerful breath for 1–3 minutes.

This exercise works the lungs, heart, and thyroid. It's good to do when you have a headache. Do this exercise when you feel uptight, depressed, lethargic, or if you have anger you can't express.

FIGURE 1

FIGURE 2

EXERCISE 2

Your hands are in Bear Grip at throat level. Your left hand faces away from you. Your right hands faces you. Hook the fingers. As you inhale, your head turns left as the hands go right (FIGURE 2). As you exhale, your head turns right as the hands go left. 3 minutes.

This exercise works on the thyroid gland and Throat Center. It also takes into account that when the thyroid secretes, the pituitary also secretes and the entire glandular system comes into balance.

EXERCISE 3

Extend your arms at a 60 degree angle to the left, the fingers of the right hand on the mounds of the left. The right upper arm crosses the mouth (FIGURE 3). Inhale deeply. Exhale through the mouth as you pull your belly in. Continue for up to 11 minutes. With practice, you can build this exercise up to 31 minutes. To end, inhale deeply, exhale forcefully through the nose, and hold the breath out for 15 seconds.

FIGURE 3

If done on a regular basis, this exercise can help prevent a heart attack. It's a tonic for the circulation and the entire glandular system. You will experience discomfort as your body corrects itself through this exercise. Endeavor to keep your elbows locked. Also, this exercise powerfully stimulates the Throat Center.

TAKE ME AS WHITE WAVES TAKE THE SAND
TO YOUR KINGDOM ON THE OTHER SHORE.
IF OUR UNION IS A ONE NIGHT STAND,
MAY THE RESTLESS SUN RISE NO MORE.

SEQUENCE 3

EXERCISE 1

Cow Pose. You're on your hands and knees with the head up and stomach down (FIGURE 1). Focus at the Third Eye. Breath of Fire. 5 minutes.

FIGURE 1

FIGURE 2

EXERCISE 2

Keep the Breath of Fire going and assume Cat Pose. Drop your head and curve your spine (FIGURE 2). Continue for 5 minutes.

> *Breath of Fire in Cat and Cow poses constitutes a tune-up for the glandular system.*
> *The glands are the guardians of your physical and mental health.*

EXERCISE 3

Yoga Mudra. Sit on your heels and lower your forehead to the ground. Interlace your fingers at the small of the back. Pull the arms off the back (FIGURE 3). Long Deep Breathing. 1–3 minutes.

Yoga Mudra revitalizes the nerves and reinstates the flow of energy and cerebral-spinal fluid through the base of the skull, an area that gets blocked from habitual use of marijuana and other drugs. This is a good exercise for mental clarity and creativity.

FIGURE 3

EXERCISE 1

Inhale through a curled tongue. Exhale through the nose (FIGURE 1). Keep your tongue extended even on the exhale. 3–11 minutes.

MODIFICATION: If you can't curl your tongue, breathe over the extended tongue.

This is called Sitali Pranayam. It assists in opening the Throat Center, ridding the body of toxins, and making an angry disposition calm. Ancient Yogic texts extoll the virtue of this breath: "That wise Yogi who daily drinks the ambrosial air by practicing Sitali Pranayam destroys fatigue, fever, decay, and old age."

FIGURE 1

FIGURE 2

EXERCISE 2

The heels of the hands are meeting at throat level. The fingers frame the face. Curl and extend your tongue (FIGURE 2). Do Breath of Fire through the curled tongue. 1–3 minutes. Next, bring the tongue in, inhale through your nose, hold the breath, and put isometric pressure on the heels of the hands at throat level for 15 seconds. Be sure your neck is in Neck Lock while holding the breath.

This exercise amplifies the benefits of the previous one.

EXERCISE 3

The right hand rests in the left. Both palms face up, at the level of the sternum. The right thumb crosses the left. The elbows are at the base of the ribs, forearms angling up so the hands are at sternum level away from the body (FIGURE 3).

Your eyes are ¹/₁₀ open, looking down towards the tip of the nose. Inhale deeply and chant the following full blast:

Ra   Ma-a... Da   Sa   Sa   Sa-y...   So Hung

This means:

**SUN MOON EARTH INFINITY
I AM THAT INFINITY
I BELONG TO AND CONTAIN**

Do this for 11 minutes. You can eventually build up to 31 minutes.

FIGURE 3

This is called Meditation to Heal All Sickness. It will make you healthy and pave the way for positive changes in your life. The mantra balances the Tattwas, which are the elements Earth, Water, Fire, Air, and Ether. According to Yoga, this balance is a prerequisite for vibrant health. By doing this mantra loudly, you're activating the Throat Center, supplying added potency to the technique.

GROUP F
SEQUENCE 1

————— ◆◇◆ —————

EXERCISE 1

Standing. Interlace your fingers behind your back. Inhale, raising your arms off your back as you lift the right knee (FIGURE 1). Exhale as you lower the arms and leg. Repeat, raising the left knee. Breathe powerfully. 3 minutes.

This exercise helps the cardiovascular system. It makes energy available to the process furthered by the subsequent exercises. It also stimulates a point on the underside of the big toes that relates to the pituitary gland and by association, the Third Eye.

FIGURE 1

FIGURE 2

EXERCISE 2

Immediately come into Crow Pose. Interlace your fingers, invert your hands, and extend your arms straight up (FIGURE 2). Close your eyes and try to see through the top of the head. Inhale through the nose. Exhale through a rounded mouth. Inhale through a rounded mouth. Exhale through the nose. Continue for 1–3 minutes.

MODIFICATION: If you cannot maintain a squatting position, be on your toes with the heels off the ground, or sit on your heels with the toes curled under.

Crow Pose relates to your earth element, which is your base. The breathing gives you an experience of your etheric self. We need to ground ourselves in order to fly. Without the earth there can be no sky.

EXERCISE 3

Sit on the floor with your legs extended. Support yourself with your hands just behind the hips. Raise your left leg (FIGURE 3). Breath of Fire. 1 minute. Switch sides and then repeat.

FIGURE 3

This exercise accesses energy at the navel for use in meditation.

DESTINY'S DICE
ARE SMOOTH ON ALL SIDES
IN THE CASINO
WHERE THE PRAYER OF THE SOUL
IS APPROVED.

EXERCISE 1

Interlace your fingers overhead. The arms are rounded. The hands are over the back of the head (posterior fontanel). (FIGURE 1). Turn your eyes all the way up. Try to see your hands through the top of the head. Long Deep Breathing. 3 minutes.

To end, inhale and hold the breath for 15 seconds. Press the underside of the tongue against the roof of the mouth. Try to pull the hands apart somewhat. Then relax the breath, lower the arms, and meditate at the brow, breathing very slowly for 1 minute.

FIGURE 1

FIGURE 2

EXERCISE 2

Assume the same pose, but this time the thumbs are pressed together, pointing straight back (FIGURE 2). Again, Long Deep Breathing for 3 minutes.

To end, inhale and hold the breath for 15 seconds. Press the underside of the tongue against the roof of the mouth. Try to pull the hands apart somewhat. Then relax the breath, lower the arms, and meditate at the brow, breathing very slowly for 1 minute.

Exercise 3

Raise the arms as before. Now the thumbs are pressed together and the index fingers are extended and point straight up (FIGURE 3). Long Deep Breathing. Deeply imbibe the light of the breath. Let it fill and fulfill you. 1 minute.

Maintain the pose. Breath of Fire. 1 minute. Continue the Breath of Fire and extend the arms to 60 degrees for 1 more minute (FIGURE 4).

To end, inhale and hold the breath for 15 seconds. Press the underside of the tongue against the roof of the mouth. Relax the breath, lower the arms, and meditate. Intone "Sat Nam" as silence streams by.

FIGURE 3

FIGURE 4

The preceding sequence worked on the pineal gland and its associate center called the Shushura, Thousand-Petalled Lotus, 10th Gate, Seat of the Soul, among other names. This center relates to Cosmic Consciousness, which is the experience of Infinity beyond words. The pineal gland regulates our seasonal and life rhythms. Birds have a similar organ which gives them sensitivity to fluctuations in the earth's magnetic field and thus aids them in migration. The "higher octave" of this function, as it relates to humans, is the navigation of the soul on its long journey home.

SEQUENCE 3

———◆◇◆———

EXERCISE 1

Block your right nostril with the right thumb. The other fingers are pointing straight up (FIGURE 1). Inhale through the left nostril. Hold the breath and intone "Wahay Guru," pumping the navel 16 times. Then block the left nostril with the right little finger and exhale through the right nostril. Time open.

According to Yogi Bhajan, "If you can do this meditation for 62 minutes and, ultimately, 2 1/2 hours, it will give you Nao Niddhi, Athara Siddhi, nine precious virtues, and 18 occult powers. The entire Universe is contained in those 27 facets. In the known Science of Yoga, among the 20 types of Yoga and their subsets, including Kundalini Yoga, this is the highest Kriya. If you can discipline yourself to do this 2 1/2 hours a day, it will make you a super person. It purifies and perfects and will make you Saintly, successful, and second to none."

FIGURE 1

Breathing through the left nostril activates the right brain hemisphere, putting you in a meditative, mellow mode. Wahay Guru is a mantra of ecstasy and Supreme Higher Consciousness. Pulsating the mantra at the navel gives it added impetus to serve as a catalyst for transformation. The number 16, in this case, relates to the Ajna Chakra, known as the Third Eye.

EXERCISE 2

Do Breath of Fire through puckered lips (FIGURE 2). 3 minutes.

Breathing through puckered lips stimulates the parasympathetic nervous system,
giving you a sense of mellow expansiveness. Breath of Fire, on the other hand, is energizing.
Combined, these components make for an interesting polarity.

FIGURE 2

FIGURE 3

EXERCISE 3

Put your hands on your shoulders, fingers in front, thumbs in back (FIGURE 3).
Gaze up at your forehead as if it were a screen. Time open.

You may see colors or scenes from your past. Don't get caught up in it. Be the witness.
Given the opportunity, our minds will sometimes go to dramatic lengths to filter out negativity
and stress. Let it go so that you can live in Truth gracefully.

STRIKE THE POLARITY
OF THAT ACTIVITY
UNTO INFINITY

Sequence 4

Exercise 1

Hold onto your knees while grinding your stomach (Figure 1). Pivot on the pelvis. Create a heat in the lower spine. Do this 11 times in one direction only.

This gives you access to navel energy to make the following exercises more effective.

Figure 1

Figure 2

Exercise 2

Inhale nose, exhale (rounded) mouth, inhale mouth, exhale nose (Figure 2). Do this breathing pattern 11 times.

This breathing pattern reverses the spin of the Third Eye and back again to open up the Higher Centers. This breath will make you feel timeless.

Note: To create a powerful set unto itself, you can do Sequence 4 up to seven times. Relax on your back after each cycle.

EXERCISE 3

Inhale deeply through the nose and chant this mantra:

WHA HAY GU RU

Do this in four separate syllables, once per breath, 11 times (FIGURE 3).

*Wahay Guru is one of the most powerful
Names of the Infinite.
For those who have been blessed with a Destiny,
this mantra is the coin of the realm.*

FIGURE 3

THE SEQUENCES IN GROUP F
ARE AN EXCELLENT
PREPARATION FOR DEEP MEDITATION.

CHAPTER 7

LOVE YOUR LIVER

The following set works on the liver. The liver is responsible for purifying the blood. It's the only organ which can regenerate itself. According to Yoga, when the liver is overtaxed, one tends to get angry a lot, or, when anger is an unresolved issue, one has an increased propensity for liver dysfunction.

Over-consumption of fried foods, alcohol, and sweets, as well as overeating, all compromise the liver. Even if our diet is perfect, the polluted air most of us breathe impinges on the liver. If done on a regular basis, the following set will help your liver keep you pure.

EXERCISE 1

Lie on your left side. Prop your head up with the left hand. Raise the right leg. Hold onto the right instep, heel, or toes (FIGURE 1). Breath of Fire. 4 minutes.

FIGURE 1

This exercise works the Liver Meridian to stimulate the liver to cleanse itself.

EXERCISE 2

Wheel Pose. Lie on your back with your feet flat, knees bent. Your hands are under the shoulders, fingers pointing back towards the feet. Arch up (FIGURE 2). Inhale through the nose, exhale nose. Then, inhale through the mouth, exhale mouth. Continue this breathing pattern for 4 minutes.

MODIFICATION: If you cannot do Wheel Pose, try Bridge Pose instead: feet flat, knees bent, hips up, elbows straight, head back (FIGURE 3). You can press your shoulders up to form a cushion for your neck.

Wheel Pose, in conjunction with this unique breathing pattern, balances the energy at the solar plexus area to restore healthy functioning to the liver.

FIGURE 2

FIGURE 3

EXERCISE 3

Repeat Exercise 1 (FIGURE 1). 2 minutes.

"Why repeat the same side?" you may ask. The answer is that sometimes we need to create a temporary imbalance to promote a more powerful and enduring balance.

EXERCISE 4

Standing. Your legs are hip to shoulder-width apart. Lean forward so that your back is parallel to the floor. Raise your head. Press your arms through the legs behind you (FIGURE 4). Arms are parallel, palms up. Feel the stretch on the right side beneath the lower ribs (where the liver is). Hold this position for 1 minute, then curl and extend your tongue and do Breath of Fire through the curled tongue for 3 more minutes.

This exercise simply puts a pressure on the liver to release toxins.
The breathing accentuates and quickens the detoxification process.

EXERCISE 5

Assume the position of the first exercise (FIGURE 1) yet again. Breathe powerfully through rounded lips. You're taking complete breaths. The inhale and exhale take about 3–4 seconds each. 30 seconds.

In combination with the previous exercises, this helps to purify the blood.

FIGURE 4

FIGURE 5

EXERCISE 6

Stand up and sit cross-legged without using your hands (FIGURE 5). Go hard and fast. Get angry! 26–52 times.

Exercise 6 is great for overcoming inertia and turning anger into inspiration.
It balances the energy at the solar plexus and promotes healthy circulation.

EXERCISE 7

Standing. Feet are shoulder-width apart. Put your hands on your hips and rotate your torso in large circles (FIGURE 6). 2 minutes.

This movement massages the liver. If you feel dizzy, nauseated, or light-headed during this, it simply means that your liver and gall bladder are detoxifying. You can do this exercise up to 11 minutes twice a day to cleanse and regenerate your liver.

FIGURE 6

EXERCISE 8

Meditate on "Sat Nam," breathing long and light (time open), choose a meditation from Chapter 13 and/or 14, chant any mantra from Appendix 3 that you're familiar with, or with a Golden Temple tape (see Appendix 3).

CHAPTER 8

STRONG AS STEEL, STEADY AS STONE

TWO SETS FOR NERVE STRENGTH

Kundalini Yoga has been called the Yoga of Nerve Strength. When our nerves are strong, we're resilient, capable, calm in a crisis, and have the capacity to turn adversity into adventure, negativity into positivity. A strong nervous system is also a prerequisite for the process of Kundalini. When you put an insignificant lump of coal under pressure, it becomes a diamond. In much the same way, when we put ourselves under conscious pressure through work on ourselves, *we* crystalize into a diamond of dimensions, able to excise stress from our lives, a living radiance of inestimable worth to all beings.

The use of drugs and an unhealthy diet compromise the nervous system. Certain patterns of self-destructive and neurotic behavior take their toll on the nervous system as well, not to mention the everyday stresses of living. To paraphrase Picasso, the mark of a genius is the ability to do the average thing when everyone else is going crazy. At this time in the history of humanity, when so much is in transition, and general confusion and spiritual malaise are rampant, people need models of steadiness and strength to emulate. Practice these two sets so that you can lead the way to a brighter day for all.

NOTE: UNLESS OTHERWISE SPECIFIED,
RELAX AFTER EVERY EXERCISE.
DO SOME WARM-UPS FROM CHAPTERS 4–6
BEFORE YOU BEGIN.

EXERCISE 1

Extend your arms out to the sides, index fingers curled under the thumbs, palms facing down (FIGURE 1). Long Deep Breathing. 5 minutes.

This exercise works the sciatic nerve in the arms as a tie-in to the entire nervous system. Your shoulders will hurt, but go through it. The breathing, of course, helps the nerves to regenerate.

EXERCISE 2

Back Platform Pose. Legs straight. Hips up. Arms straight (FIGURE 2). Long Deep Breathing. 3–5 minutes. Immediately move to the next exercise.

MODIFICATION: If Back Platform Pose proves too difficult, you can substitute Bridge Pose (Back Platform Pose with knees bent, feet flat).

FIGURE 1

FIGURE 2

Back Platform Pose puts pressure on the nervous system to release the deeper pressure of accumulated stress. This is also a very good exercise for the heart. Initially, you may feel that you can't maintain the pose. Don't let that impulse stop you. It's only a subjective response to an objective process. Be willing to die a small death for life forever!

EXERCISE 3

Have your legs straight, feet flexed. Reach forward and pull back on the toes (FIGURE 3). Use your arm strength to stretch. Let everything else remain relaxed. If you feel strain in your hips and/or lower back, you need to ease up. Breath of Fire. 3 minutes.

MODIFICATION: If you can't reach your feet, hold your ankles calves or knees.

This stretch works the sciatic nerve and as a counter pose to the previous exercise.
Breath of Fire helps to facilitate the release of stress from the previous two exercises and oxygenates the body to enhance the subsequent exercises in this sequence.

FIGURE 3

FIGURE 4

EXERCISE 4

Sit on your heels in Rock Pose (FIGURE 4). Inhale. Exhale. Hold the breath out. Pump the stomach as long as you can with the breath held out. Do this 11 times.

Holding the breath out while pumping the stomach assists in oxygenation of the nerves, helps the heart, and regenerates the adrenals.

EXERCISE 5

Repeat Exercise 2 (FIGURE 2).

FIGURE 5

EXERCISE 6

Standing. Bend your knees slightly. Lean forward. Your hands are holding the area just above the inner knee (FIGURE 5). In this position, pump the stomach with the breath held out as in Exercise 4.

> WE MAY HAVE TO DIE
> SOMETIME
> BUT NEED NOT GROW OLD.

EXERCISE 7

Sit comfortably with your spine straight (FIGURE 6). Have your eyes ¹/₁₀ open, looking down towards the tip of the nose. Chant the mantra:

Wa Hay   Gu-Ru   Sat   Nam   Haree   Haree   Ram   Ram

Wa Hay   Gu-Ru   Sat   Nam   Haree   Haree   Ram   Ram

FIGURE 6

NOTE: SEE THE FOLLOWING PAGE
FOR THE MECHANICS OF THIS MEDITATION.

◇ As you chant "Wahay Guru," squeeze the rectum muscle and feel the sound resonate there.

◇ As you chant "Sat Nam," squeeze the sex organ muscle (keeping the rectum contracted) and feel the sound resonate in that area.

◇ As you chant "Haree Haree," (The "R" in Haree is pronounced almost like a "D") pull the navel in and feel the sound resonate there.

◇ As you chant "Ram Ram," pull the diaphragm up under the ribs and feel the sound resonate at the sternum.

Then go through it again, but this time:

◇ As you chant "Wahay Guru," relax the diaphragm and feel the sound resonate at the throat.

◇ As you chant "Sat Nam," relax the navel and feel the sound resonate at the Third Eye (on a line between the eyebrows, an inch above the bridge of the nose).

◇ As you chant "Haree Haree," relax the sex organ muscle and feel the sound resonate at the top of the head.

◇ As you chant "Ram Ram," relax the rectum and feel the sound resonate above the top of the head.

This meditation takes some practice to do as instructed. Each of the sounds that comprise this mantra is a potent Name of the Infinite. This technique will help put your "lower self" in the context of the Higher. In this process we don't want to repress anything; instead we want to transform it.

THOSE WHO PRACTICE THE ART
OF FEARLESS SURRENDER
HAVE TORN THEIR CALENDARS
TO THE END OF DAYS;
THEIR EXISTENCE
IS ONLY TO PRAISE.

SET TWO

This is a profound sequence which will regenerate the nerves and strengthen your digestive system and lower back. In releasing blocks in the lower centers (rectum, sex organ, navel point), you are freed from a false sense of self.

NOTE: PRECEDE THIS SET WITH SET ONE IN THIS
CHAPTER OR ONE OR MORE OF THE WARM-UP SEQUENCES
FROM CHAPTERS 4–6.

EXERCISE 1

Sit on your left heel. Keep your hips square. Extend your right leg. Wrap the first two fingers of both hands around the right big toe. Angle forward, elongate your lower spine. Pull your chin back (FIGURE 1). Hold this position perfectly still with a normal breath, applying a constant Mul Bhand, contracting the muscles of the anal sphincter, sex organ, and navel. 3 minutes. Inhale. Exhale, hold the breath out completely, and squeeze the lower muscles. Hold the breath out as long as you can. Do this twice more, for a total of three times.

MODIFICATION: If you cannot sit on your heel, have the left foot against the inside of the right thigh.

FIGURE 1

This exercise is called Maha Mudra. It's actually one of the most potent exercises in Yoga. It's said this exercise can heal anything. If you do this as an exercise unto itself, do one side (start with 3 minutes and build up the time to 7½ minutes), relax on your back, then do the other side for an equal amount of time and relax again. In the context of this sequence, we isolate the right side in order to strengthen the nerves (the left side relates to the glands).

EXERCISE 2

Kundalini Lotus Pose. Wrap the first two fingers of each hand around the corresponding big toe or hold onto your insteps or heels. Extend your legs up and out. Balance on your sacrum (FIGURE 2). Apply Mul Bhand. Squeeze the lower muscles as in the previous exercise. Hold this pose with normal breathing for 3 minutes. Inhale. Exhale, hold the breath out completely, and squeeze the lower muscles. Hold the breath out as long as you can. Do this twice more. Immediately move to the next exercise.

MODIFICATION: Hold under your knees or support yourself with your hands.

Kundalini Lotus adjusts the sacrum, and transmutes bottled-up energy from the lower nerve plexi.

FIGURE 2

FIGURE 3

EXERCISE 3

Your legs are together and extended straight. Pull back on your toes. Try to sit up straight, holding onto the toes. Pull your chin back like a soldier at attention (FIGURE 3). Long Deep Breathing. 3 minutes. Inhale. Exhale, hold the breath out as long as you can, apply Mul Bhand. Do this twice more.

This one can be done as an exercise unto itself
to correct sexual dysfunctions in men.

EXERCISE 4

Back Platform Pose. Hips up, head back, arms straight, legs straight (FIGURE 4). Hold this position with a normal breath (do not apply Mul Bhand) for 3 minutes. Then inhale, exhale, and hold the breath out as long as you can, squeezing the lower muscles. Do it twice more for a total of 3 times.

MODIFICATION: Have your feet flat and knees bent.

This pose creates stress to help you form an immunity against it.
It also stimulates the Triple Warmer Meridian, which regulates respiration,
digestion, and elimination.

FIGURE 4

FIGURE 5

EXERCISE 5

Assume a front push-up position. Your toes are not curled under (FIGURE 5). Do 26 push-ups at a moderate pace with a deep breath, inhaling up, exhaling down. Move immediately to the next exercise.

MODIFICATION: Have your knees on the ground.

The nerves control the muscles. In this case, we're working the muscles to strengthen the nerves.
This exercise helps to stimulate the nerves at the solar plexus—all 72,000 of them.

EXERCISE 6

Elbow Platform Pose. Your legs are extended in front of you. You're on your elbows with your hands in fists at armpit level. Raise your body off the ground so you're supporting yourself on your elbows and heels only. Drop your head back (FIGURE 6). Long Deep Breathing. 1–3 minutes. Inhale, then exhale and hold the breath out, squeezing the lower muscles (1 time only). Inhale deeply and relax.

MODIFICATION: Have the forearms on the ground as well.

Elbow Platform Pose strengthens the heart and nerves. It will give you an opportunity to test your grit. Pressure on the elbows helps your stomach.

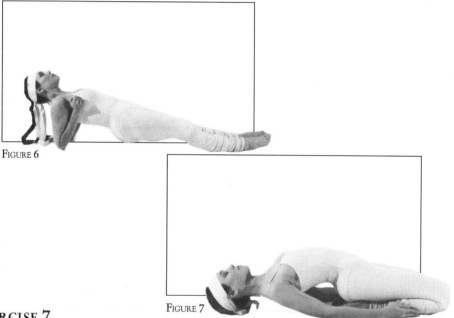

FIGURE 6

FIGURE 7

EXERCISE 7

Sit on your heels. Lie back so that your upper back and head are on the floor. Keep your knees on the floor, no wider than the hips. Squeeze the lower muscles. Maintain Mul Bhand as you breathe long and deeply (FIGURE 7). 3 minutes. Inhale. Exhale and hold the breath out completely and squeeze the lower muscles. Hold the breath out as long as you can. Do this twice more. Take your time coming out of this pose.

MODIFICATION: Lean back on your forearms, or support yourself with your hands. Otherwise, have the soles of the feet together and lie on your back.

This exercise can help correct digestive problems. It's not easy to maintain Mul Bhand and breathe at the same time. Practice makes perfect.

EXERCISE 8

Frog Pose. Do 30 repetitions somewhat slowly with a deep breath. Inhale up (FIGURE 9). Exhale down (FIGURE 8).

FIGURE 8   FIGURE 9

In the context of this sequence, Frog Pose helps to circulate vital energy throughout the body to help the nerves regenerate. Overall, Frog Pose will make you a more potent person.

FIGURE 10

EXERCISE 9

Lie on your back. As you inhale, raise the right leg straight up, simultaneously squeezing a slight Mul Bhand. Exhale as you lower the leg and relax Mul Bhand. Do the same thing raising the left leg. Do these alternate leg lifts for 3 minutes (FIGURE 10). As you raise the leg, flex the foot; as you lower it, point the toes.

This exercise balances the energy in the body and helps the digestive system.

EXERCISE 10—MEDITATION TO DISCOVER YOUR TRUE IDENTITY

Reality can only be expressed
in terms of negation.

–Alfred North Whitehead

Sit with your legs crossed (FIGURE 11). We're going to disabuse ourselves of the encrustations of ego which false personality has fostered upon us. Do this: conjure up every identity you consider yourself to be or can be related to as (i.e., man, woman, Republican, Democrat, artist, lover, etc.). Negate each of these with the awareness that you are the Identity which gives rise to all the temporary ones. Time open.

FIGURE 11

When energy is blocked in the lower centers, it translates into a false sense of self.
For instance, someone may think he's a cross between Rambo and Clint Eastwood, when in reality
he's an overweight truckdriver with a drinking problem. Work on ourselves can be initially
painful because it strips away our illusions. That pain is more than compensated for as the energy
of Spirit leads you to the Awareness that you are an essence in essence, unique in the Universe,
and in effect, on a mission from God!

CHAPTER 9

◦◇◦

PAST TENSE,
FUTURE PERFECT

TWO SETS FOR
OVERCOMING HIDDEN AGENDAS

QUESTION: Why are our parents so good at pushing our buttons?
ANSWER: Because they installed them.

Hidden agendas are modes of behavior initially instituted early in our lives as strategies to get attention, love, or simply (in our own minds) to survive. What begins as an affectation or expected response is encoded into us over time to become a pattern which usually leads to failure.

During adulthood, hidden agendas are transformed into an indirect means of compensating for emotional lack. The indirect means of continually trying to relive something we experienced directly leads to what could be seen as neurotic behavior. Hidden agendas are like software bugs. We need to rewrite our programs.

Here are some common hidden agendas. I'm sure all of us can identify with one or more of these:

1. The need to control or be controlled
2. The need to be the center of attention
3. A deep-seated authority problem
4. Fear of intimacy
5. Fear of being rejected or unloved
6. Fear of death which colors all one's behavior
7. The need to try and capture or destroy the image of one or both of our parents in relationships
8. Lack of self-worth

Set One

Exercise 1

Sit cross-legged. Hold your knees. Arch your spine, feel a powerful pressure under the shoulder blades (13th, 14th, and 15th vertebrae). Press your head back to follow the curve of the spine (Figure 1). Inhale, exhale, hold the breath out, pump your stomach vigorously for 15 seconds. Do this five more times. Relax or meditate before going on.

Stimulation of the 13th, 14th, and 15th vertebrae pressurizes the liver. Pumping the stomach with the breath held out in this pose helps begin to unravel deep emotional duress buried in the solar plexus area. The faster you pump the stomach, the more effective this exercise will be.

Figure 1

Figure 2

Exercise 2

Press your hands together (away from the body) at sternum level, forearms parallel to the ground, right thumb crossed over left. As in the previous exercise, pressurize your spine under the shoulder blades, head tilted back to follow the curve of the spine (Figure 2). Take four deep breaths, exhale, hold out, and pump the navel powerfully for 15–20 seconds. Do this up to five more times. Relax or meditate before continuing.

This pose is known as Abeah Kriya. It will help regulate the entire nervous system, deliver you to a state of inner balance, and can prevent depression and other negative emotions.

Note: Do this set on an empty stomach.

EXERCISE 3

Again curve your spine, creating a pressure under the shoulder blades. Your arms are extended straight, parallel to the ground, palms up (FIGURE 3). The inside edge of the hands and wrists (if possible) are meeting. Breathe long and deeply. Try to think negative thoughts about yourself. You'll soon find you can't. Now think positive thoughts, i.e., "I am great and graceful, beautiful and Divine," etc. 3 minutes. Relax on your back for 3 minutes before continuing.

This pose stimulates spinal serum in concert with controlled negativity
to match the frequency of the deep negativity we're trying to excise. As a result, negativity,
the saboteur of graceful existence, will stay away from you.

FIGURE 3   FIGURE 4

EXERCISE 4

As in the previous exercises, curve your spine, pressurizing the area under the shoulder blades, head tilted back to follow the curve of the spine. Extend your right arm at a slight upward angle, and pull your left hand back. The hands are open (FIGURE 4). Stretch in this position for 1½ to 3 minutes. Switch sides and repeat.

This exercise adjusts the shoulder area and your metabolism
to bring the emotions into balance.

Set Two

Try the following sequence daily for seven days straight. It will put you through changes. You're going to contact your infant self–actually a demon in disguise who never grew up–and transform it so your life can be healed.

Exercise 1

Press your hands together. The heels of the hands are pressed against the navel. The fingers are pointing forward. Very powerfully, move your hands up and down. (Figure 1). You must sweat. Put your all into it. 7 minutes.

Figure 1

Exercise 1 builds the energy field in the navel area and brings your mind to a neutral state to help you process unresolved feelings.

Exercise 2

Your arms are parallel, palms up (Figure 2). Breath of Fire. 2–3 minutes.

EXERCISE 3

Maintain the arm position (FIGURE 2). Long Deep Breathing. 2–3 minutes.

FIGURE 2

EXERCISE 4

Maintain the arm position. Tilt your head back a bit. Open-mouth breathing on both the inhale and exhale. As you exhale, sigh out your deepest pain. 2–3 minutes.

EXERCISE 5

Keep the arms up. Face forward. Inhale. Hold the breath. Pulsate your awareness from the navel to the brow over and over for 15 seconds. Inhale, repeat twice more.

EXERCISE 6

Almost there! Keep the arms up. Bring your awareness deep into your belly and contact the source of all the pain and disappointment you've felt in your life. Pull it out by the roots. Let it be burned up in the bonfire you've built at the navel. For subsequent practice, think of a visualization which works best for you. 1 minute.

The position of the arms challenges the shoulder area where rage is stored in the form of tension. It stimulates your Heart Center, a perspective from which self-healing is possible. The breathing sequence has psychological implications for the resolution of negativity, resentment, anger, and angst.

EXERCISE 7

Lower your arms. Have your hands in your lap (FIGURE 3). Go deep into yourself. Meditate on your hidden agendas and resolve them. Let bygones be bygones.

EXERCISE 8

Put your right hand on the sternum, your left hand over it, (FIGURE 4) and chant any Kundalini Yoga mantra which stirs your heart and/or try the following, which should be chanted in a monotone:

GOD & ME, ME & GOD ARE ONE
ME I THOU, THOU I ME
EK ONG KAR SAT GUR PRASAD
SAT GUR PRASAD EK ONG KAR

FIGURE 3

FIGURE 4

The grouping of these phrases and mantra is very technical and powerful.
Chanting this helps you circumvent your intellect (which takes you in circles) and opens
your heart to the fact that you are not this or that, but are that you
are, and that forever. That understanding is grounds for ecstasy, pure and simple.

CHAPTER 10

ENERGETIC SET

EXERCISE 1

Lie on your back. Your hands are under the buttocks, palms facing down for support. Do double leg lifts to and from 90 degrees (FIGURE 1). As you raise your legs, flex your feet; as you lower them, point your toes. For the duration of this exercise, do Breath of Fire through a rounded mouth. Do this for 3–5 minutes.

MODIFICATION: Keep your knees bent.

FIGURE 1

Breath of Fire through puckered lips helps detoxify you and put you in a meditative mode. The leg lifts contribute to the process of self-purification and activation of the navel center.

EXERCISE 2A

Get onto your hands and knees and begin Breath of Fire, again through a rounded mouth. Alternately raise one leg up behind you (FIGURE 2). Lower it. Repeat with the other leg. 4 minutes.

FIGURE 2

FIGURE 3

EXERCISE 2B

Without stopping, add the arms to the previous movement. As you raise the left leg, raise the right arm (FIGURE 3) and vice versa. 2 minutes. Reach with the arms.

These exercises balance the two energies, prana and apana, at the solar plexus and adjust the brain hemispheres as well.

EXERCISE 3

Do Frog Pose 52 times (FIGURES 4 and 5). Go immediately to the next exercise.

FIGURE 4   FIGURE 5

Frog Pose helps pump energy up to the Higher Centers.

FIGURE 6   FIGURE 7

EXERCISE 4

Sit on your heels. As you inhale, raise your arms straight up with the palms facing in (FIGURE 6). As you exhale, lower the arms to 60 degrees with the palms facing out (FIGURE 7). Continue at a moderate pace with a powerful breath for 5 minutes. Immediately move on.

This works the upper magnetic field, lungs, and lymphatic system.

EXERCISE 5

Sit cross-legged (FIGURE 8). Breathe long and deeply through the nose. 5 minutes.

FIGURE 8

*This helps neutralize the toxins and tension you brought
up from deep places in the previous exercises.*

EXERCISE 6

Practice a Meditation as given in Chapter 13 and/or 14 and/or chant any Kundalini Yoga mantra. (See Appendix 3.)

CHAPTER 11

MASTERING YOUR MOODS

Almost all of us have been let down or hurt. This often becomes a pattern because our programming stems from inurement to rejection. Living on the defensive or resisting any kind of relationship altogether puts life in a holding pattern. Success in life depends on your capacity for intimacy, to feel the Universe in you and accept its blessings. This set helps to overcome paranoia so that you can trust and open yourself to loving and being loved.

CURRENCY

Generation after generation
Telegraph a legacy
Of pain
To innocent offspring–
Now we will honor each other,
Love again,
And cancel
Our appointments with fate;
We must,
Because "The buck stops here."
It says, "In God We Trust."

–Ravi Singh

EXERCISE 1

Extend the arms straight to the sides. The fingers are curled in, pressed against the mounds. The thumbs are pointing straight up (FIGURE 1). To the rhythm of the Breath of Fire, continuously point your thumbs forward, up, straight back, and up. You will feel the movement all the way up into the shoulders. 7–8 minutes.

This exercise works on the pituitary gland so that you can see through the mental limitations which paranoia imposes. It also balances the brain hemispheres which get imbalanced from emotional and physical abuse. This exercise also strengthens your sense of self and is good for any kind of respiratory problem. It will test you if done for the prescribed time. Go through it! You can't afford not to.

FIGURE 1

Remember, no doctor can do this for you, no therapist, no minister, no teacher. You have to do it for yourself. That's the way it should be. Sacrifice for the sake of Spirit is both a privilege and a gift. Whatever handicaps or pain our early experiences may have wrought are not our fault, but as conscious people, the ways in which these things affect our lives become our responsibility. Assumption of this responsibility will make us stronger and wiser than we ever thought we could be.

> MY PAST TENSE IS A WIDOW;
> I DIED IN THE WAR OF THE WORLDS
> AND CLIMBED THE LADDER ON FIRE.
> PATTERS AND PERSUASIONS WERE RUNGS
> SACRIFICED FOR MY ASCENSION.

EXERCISE 2

Assume the same starting position as the previous exercise (FIGURE 1). As you inhale, the thumbs come almost to the shoulders (FIGURE 2). As you exhale, snap the arms back to the original position. Breathe powerfully. 2 minutes.

FIGURE 2

This exercise also stimulates the pituitary, works on the lungs, and the stomach as well (the elbow area and the outside upper arms are stomach points).

EXERCISE 3

Hold your knees. As you inhale, press your lower back forward and stretch your neck up (FIGURE 3). As you exhale, let your lower back curve back and press your face forward (FIGURE 4). 4 minutes.

FIGURE 3

FIGURE 4

This exercise pressurizes the thyroid gland to help you master your moods.

EXERCISE 4

Put your hands on the shoulders, fingers in front, thumbs in back (FIGURE 5). As you inhale, the arms go straight to the sides (FIGURE 6). As you exhale, the hands come back to the shoulders (FIGURE 5). Then inhale as you bring the elbows up (FIGURE 7). Exhale as you return to the original position (FIGURE 5). Mentally chant the sound "Har" on every inhale and exhale. 3–4 minutes.

FIGURE 5

FIGURE 6   FIGURE 7

"Har" means the Creative Aspect of the Infinite. It's a mantra of power and prosperity. It will give you the strength and self-confidence to be able to trust. The movement of the arms stimulates the thyroid gland and balances the brain hemispheres.

EXERCISE 5

Lie on your back. The hands are under the buttocks for support. Raise your heels 6 inches off the floor (FIGURE 8). Long Deep Breathing. 1–3 minutes.

MODIFICATION: If your lower back feels unduly put-upon, raise one leg.

This exercise works on the navel for self-empowerment and stimulates the brain cells.

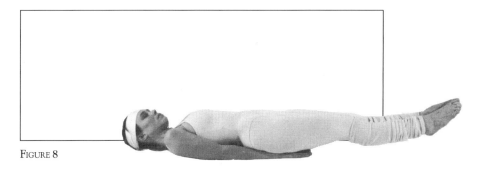

FIGURE 8

EXERCISE 6

Lie on your back. Cross your ankles. As you inhale, raise the legs straight up (FIGURE 9) and exhale while lowering the legs. 3 minutes.

MODIFICATION: If your lower back feels unduly put-upon, bend your knees.

FIGURE 9

This exercise also engenders navel power for confidence, patience, and grit. As we absorb nutrients through the workings of the digestive fire, we are able to nurture ourselves from the food of experience to grow wise. As we strengthen the navel point, painful patterns can be avoided. Crossing the ankles stimulates points relating to the kidneys and ovaries. When there is tension in the ovary area, a woman may retain water. This exercise can be useful in alleviating this.

Exercise 7

Lie on your back. Your arms are straight up, perpendicular to the ground. The fingers are pointing straight up, and the thumbs are pointing straight back. Inhale. Exhale as you sit up and touch the toes (FIGURE 10). 3–6 minutes.

FIGURE 10

This exercise works on adjusting the pelvic bone. It stimulates navel energy to facilitate the opening of the higher centers so that feelings of paranoia can defer to freedom.

Exercise 8

Bridge Pose. Head up, face forward (FIGURE 11). Inhale. Exhale as you lower your buttocks to the ground (FIGURE 12). Continue powerfully. 3–4 minutes. Immediately move to the next exercise.

FIGURE 11

FIGURE 12

This exercise pressurizes the thyroid and adjusts the hips.

Exercise 9

Come into Bridge Pose with your head back (FIGURE 13). Breathe deeply through the open mouth. 1–2 minutes. Now stick your tongue out and vibrate the back of the tongue as if you were gargling. 1 minute. Move immediately to the next one.

This exercise stimulates the parathyroid gland and thus can be considered a preventive measure against the common cold.

FIGURE 13

FIGURE 14

Exercise 10

Sit in a comfortable meditative position (FIGURE 14). Breathe long and light, as slow as a glacier, and as deep as the ocean it will someday become. 4 minutes.

When the thyroid secretes, the pituitary secretes as well.
In light of the previous exercises, you'll find yourself able to meditate very deeply now.

EXERCISE 11

Interlace your fingers overhead. The thumb tips are touching pointing back, the arms are rounded (FIGURE 15). Imagine your navel has a nose. Breathe through the navel. As you exhale, feel and imagine the space framed by the arms, around the head, is filling with light. Your eyes are $1/10$ open, looking down towards the tip of the nose. Breathe long and deep. Listen to the tape of Jap Sahib, if available (see Appendix 5 for ordering information). 9 minutes.

FIGURE 15

This exercise will give you Majesty and the strength to be the answer to your own prayers.

A WHITE BUTTERFLY
IN THE CHRYSALIS OF EVERY SOUL
WAITS FOR THE BELLS OF SPRING
TO TOLL.

Chapter 12

❖

QUICK FIXES

TEN TIMELY 3-MINUTE TECHNIQUES TO PUT YOU BACK ON TRACK

No one can readily change the weather, but we can clear away the clouds of various forms of stress putting a damper on our day. These simple techniques can make a definite difference in your day and possibly your life!

HOW TO TURN ANGER INTO INSPIRATION

Anger is not a bad thing; in fact, it's a great motivator, but we have to learn to channel it creatively.

Make your hands into fists and thrust your elbows back past the plane of the body. Press your chest out. Take five deep breaths, inhale deep, hold the breath, and punch (FIGURE 1). Get mad! When you can't hold the breath any longer, exhale. Inhale, repeat a powerful punching motion with the breath held twice more. Then sit, eyes closed, and breathe as slowly as you can for 2 minutes. Rise and shine.

FIGURE 1

HELPING CLEAR FEAR

According to the tradition of yoga, there are three levels of fear: fear of being rejected, fear of being unloved, and fear of dying. Ultimately, we have already been judged infinitely acceptable, infinitely desirable, and what we truly are is Infinity itself. Therefore, there is nothing to fear.

Fear manifests itself in the body as an imbalance in the water element. In a state of abject fear, a person sheds tears, sweats, and loses control of the bladder. When you're feeling fearful about something, do this:

Sit in a chair or on the floor with your legs crossed. Lean forward and gently pound the kidney area for about a minute with your hands in loose fists (FIGURE 2).

Then sit up straight, close your eyes and localize your awareness at the navel point. Visualize and feel a sun inside the body behind the navel. As you inhale, the sun gets hotter, and as you exhale, it gets brighter. 2 minutes.

FIGURE 2

I WANT TO BE LOST IN YOUR INFINITE AZURE—
AMELIA SOARING INTO THE ONE SUN.

Energizing the Late Afternoon Lows

The transition from afternoon to evening creates a glitch in the psyche. To prevent depression or energy loss, one needs to compensate. Most people repair to the nearest bar for happy hour. Having a couple of drinks or a candy bar may get you through the day, but in the long run, this approach has a definite down-side. Conscious breathing is a very effective means of energizing.

Raise your arms straight out to the sides and up to a 60 degree angle. The fingers are pressing against the mounds (at the tops of the palms) and the thumbs are up (FIGURE 3). Breath of Fire. 2–3 minutes.

Inhale, hold the breath, and quickly move the fingers over and under the thumbs for 15 seconds, then with the hands in the original position, slowly bring your thumbs towards one another overhead. Let your thumbs meet, then slowly lower your arms as you relax the breath, feeling a rainbow of radiance described by the arc of the descending thumbs. Sit for a minute breathing slowly. Feel bright and beautiful.

FIGURE 3

This exercise is extremely energizing.
It also gives you charisma and radiance. Accordingly, it's good to do before
an interview or before you go out in the morning.

DELETING DEPRESSION

Most people accept periodic depression pretty much as an accepted fact of life. These simple techniques will help make a bad mood good.

Inhale through puckered lips, hold briefly, then exhale forcefully through the nose. Do this ten times. Now go about your day in a great way!

Here's another anti-depression measure:

1. Drink a glass of water.

2. Check which nostril is more open (every 2½ hours one nostril predominates) and block it with the thumb of the corresponding hand. The fingers point straight up (FIGURE 4). Breathe deeply through the other nostril for 3 minutes.

FIGURE 4

NOTE: IF THE DEPRESSION YOU EXPERIENCE
IS CHRONIC OR SEVERE,
DON'T HESITATE TO SEEK PROFESSIONAL HELP.

What to Do When Hefty Headaches Happen

A headache is your body's way of getting attention, of telling you something's getting out of hand. Some of the causes for headaches are: overall tension interdicting blood flow to the brain, a toxic condition in the body, or the signal for a spinal, neck, or cranial adjustment (consider a sojourn to your favorite chiropractor).

So the next time sledgehammers start up in your skull, try this sequence. If headaches are chronic or severe, consult a physician immediately.

1. Inhale as you raise your shoulders up towards the ears, and exhale as you lower them (FIGURE 5). Continue powerfully for 1 minute.

2. Neck rolls, taking about 8 seconds per complete turn. Follow the course of your collarbone (FIGURE 6). Do this seven times, then reverse direction and repeat.

3. Press your thumbs hard under the cheekbones for 1 minute.

Other headache remedies are: soak your feet in cold running water; drink lots of water during the day; find fresh air and liberally partake.

FIGURE 5

FIGURE 6

According to Yoga, another cause for headaches (even migraines) is the accumulation of mucus in the body. Mucus gathers in the back of the throat overnight. To prevent it from collecting in the body, Yogis do the following upon arising in the morning: Using a potassium, alum, and salt tooth powder (to order, call 619/281-1327), brush the back of your tongue until you gag. You will be able to spit out the mucous that's collected in the back of the throat. This seems extreme but it's actually very good for you. Yoga claims this practice makes the eyes water and thus helps prevent cataracts and can help prevent arthritis.

MANIFESTING MORPHEUS (SLEEP CURES)

When it's late and sleep is something you can only dream of, try the following:

❖ Wash your feet in cold running water.

❖ Comb your hair forward and back a few times, with a wooden comb. This will help take your energy out of its active mode.

❖ Block your right nostril with your right thumb and breathe long and deep through the left nostril. Do this until you feel sleepy.

TURNING THE TABLES ON TEMPTATION

You just started a serious diet three days ago and you're at your best friend's wedding and they're cutting that luscious, creamy cake. The ubiquitous dark angel of rationalization is whispering sweet nothings in your ear. What to do?!

Inhale, hold the breath as long as you comfortably can. Then exhale the desire you're trying to overcome. Do this till reason wins out over impulse.

This exercise stimulates the parasympathetic nervous system which gives you a sense of serenity. From that place of overview, you can act with impunity in doing what's best for you.

HOW TO DECIDE

If you are in conflict, or have to make a tough decision, make a list:

1. Your personal choice

2. Your sentimental, temperamental, emotional choice

3. Your conscious choice

If you're willing to be honest with yourself, this writing exercise is a surprisingly quick way to gain clarity and insight regarding any situation.

Even the most spiritual people have conflicts. What makes them great is that they've created a habit of unwaveringly making the conscious choice once they know what it is. You have the capacity for Mastery. Let your criterion be the conscious path. Always choose that which exalts you, even if you have to sacrifice some initial ego gratification. Live and think consciously and you can never go wrong. Conscious choices don't mean making decisions in which you feel you have to be a martyr to yourself. Feel the flow of Spirit in you. Celebrate it; it's real. Let the tender kiss of Spirit wake you after the long night of slumber.

How to Reconnect with Your Essence

Sometimes we get so caught up in the play of the mundane that we lose sight of the big picture. This technique can help you remember not to forget that you are you, and that forever.

Cross your forearms just above the wrists in front of the sternum, left forearm in front. The index fingers and thumbtips are meeting on both hands. The palms of the hands face the body (FIGURE 7). Your eyes are $1/10$ open, looking down towards the tip of the nose. Inhale. Exhale. Hold the breath out and intone:

HAREE HAREE HAREE HAREE HAREE HAREE HAREE

As you hold the breath out, pump the stomach while mentally chanting. On the first breath, mentally chant three times. On the second breath do it four times, and on the third breath do it five times. Then sit still for another $1\frac{1}{2}$ minutes and feel your Forever Self.

FIGURE 7

Meditation for Majesty

Very often, because of lack of self-esteem, we feel we have to overcompensate to have others accept us. We wind up giving away our power. This simple inner affirmation will trigger the Tenth Body (see Appendix 2 on the Ten Bodies) so that you can live in the radiance of the Great Victorious Light which is truly you. Say the following to yourself before you get within nine feet (the size of a healthy human aura, and thus sphere of influence) of the person with whom you'll interact:

I Will Be Noble

Once is all it takes!

Provenance

The First Word
Led to its twin,
Enamored of its echo
I went within.
The wind drove
Through the canopy,
A wild power ensued–
Why am I here?
So a there is True.

The face of the firmament
Dawned,
When I opened the locket
Of my heart to You.

–Ravi Singh

BREATHINGS

SEGMENTED BREATH FOR ENERGY AND FOCUS

Your hands are framing the sternum; left hand on top, palm facing down; right hand on the bottom, palm up. Your hands are two inches in front of the body. Your eyes are $1/10$ open, looking down towards the tip of the nose (FIGURE 1).

This breath is done in increments. Inhale in eight parts ("sniffs") so that by the eighth inhale, you're filled. Exhale in eight parts, so by the eighth exhale, the breath is out. Intone "Sa-Ta-Na-Ma" twice to match the eight-part rhythm. 11 minutes.

FIGURE 1

This breath meditation bolsters the Arcline (see Appendix 2 on the Ten Bodies), which relates to powerful focus and the beaming power of the mind enhancing any subsequent meditation. Segmented breathing stimulates the pituitary gland and helps you use your full lung capacity. The ratio of breaths relates to a specific energy center or system. Eight-part breathing relates to the Heart Center. Focusing at the tip of the nose helps "capture the mind."

Anti-Stress Breath for Sophistication & Strength

Your right hand is by your right ear, as if taking an oath. Your left elbow is pressed into the left side at the base of the ribs. The left forearm is parallel to the floor and the left palm is facing up (Figure 2).

The underside of the tongue is against the roof of the mouth, the teeth are together, and your eyes are $1/10$ open, looking down towards the tip of the nose. Inhale for 15 seconds. Hold the breath for 15 seconds. Exhale for 15 seconds. Hold out for 15 seconds. You can mentally chant "Sa-Ta-Na-Ma" in a uniform rhythm to keep the duration of each breath constant. 11 minutes.

Figure 2

This one takes practice. You can begin by holding the breath in and out for 10 seconds and building up to 15. This technique can be useful against shingles and other skin disorders which can occur when the nerves near the surface of the skin aren't getting enough oxygen. It will give you incredible stamina, build your body's capacity to heal itself, bring your emotions under your control and give you super-sensitivity. As a student of Kundalini Yoga, this type of technique should be part of your repertoire.

Breath for the Immune System & Inner Talents

Block your right nostril with your right index finger. The left hand is at shoulder level, ring finger and thumbtip meeting (FIGURE 3). Do Breath of Fire through the left nostril for 11 minutes. Build the time over time to 31 minutes.

Then inhale, hold the breath for 15 seconds, and with the fingers interlaced at face level (FIGURE 4), try to pull the hands apart. Do this three more times.

Yogi Bhajan has said, "We are born with inherited strength which is equal to the power of God, but our projected strength is blocked by our own anger, self-defeat, and blame."

FIGURE 3

FIGURE 4

This breath meditation can help heal you physically and mentally. Breathing through the left nostril engenders a calming energy. Breath of Fire, on the other hand, is stimulating. The combination of these two variables creates a cool fire in the body which, according to Yoga, no virus can withstand. We're not making any claims, but if you know someone who is very sick, try to inspire them to do this meditation. By neutralizing the inner anger, this technique can help you turn handicaps into attributes as well.

Breath Meditation to Balance Yourself & Others

Interlace your fingers with both palms facing up. Your fingers are meeting fingerprint to fingerprint. The thumbs are pointing forward. Place this configuration against the navel (Figure 5).

Have your teeth pressed together, the underside of the tongue on the roof of the mouth, and your chin pulled back slightly, like a soldier at attention. Your eyes are $1/10$ open, looking to the tip of the nose. Inhale in four parts through the nose, so that by the fourth inhale, you're filled. Exhale in one part. Mentally chant "Sa-Ta-Na-Ma" as you inhale and "Wahay Guru" as you exhale. Do this for up to 31 minutes. To end inhale, turn your gaze up to the brow and hold the breath. When you need to, slowly exhale. Take some time to relax and reorient before resuming normal activity.

FIGURE 5

This technique will give you the power to heal and balance through touch. In addition, it will coordinate and enhance your mental capacities to help you be super-efficient, intuitive, and masterful. Do this 31 minutes a day for a 1,000 days without missing a day. It will make you a healer. Never forget, it's not we who do the healing, but God working through us.

METABOLIC BREATHING WITH HANDS LIKE A TEAPOT

The heels of the hands are meeting. Your left hand is in a fist. Cover the left hand with the right. The thumbs are side by side, resting on the left index finger (do not let them touch the right one). There will be a hole between the thumbs.

Your elbows are against the base of the ribs and the forearms are angling up so that the hands are eight inches in front of the mouth (FIGURE 6). Inhale through the nose. Exhale through puckered lips, directing the air through the hole created by the thumbs. 11 minutes. Feel calm, collected, directed, and perfected.

FIGURE 6

This meditation is called Chata Chya Kriya. It will help you to relax and keep you young and healthy. This is a great technique to help you wind down after a hard day. Do this one before bed for a very restful and refreshing sleep.

BREATH MEDITATION FOR OPPORTUNITIES

Your hands are pressed together firmly, fingers pointing straight up, thumbs against the sternum (FIGURE 7). Do not let the hands come apart.

Inhale, hold the breath, and mentally repeat the mantra "Wahay Guru" eight times. Exhale, hold the breath out, and again mentally repeat "Wahay Guru" eight times. Hold the breath in and out for an equal amount of time. Your eyes are $1/10$ open, looking down towards the tip of the nose. 31 minutes.

FIGURE 7

This technique engenders a powerful neutrality and magnetizes you to opportunities. Do this before bed, so that the next day can be filled with abundance and blessings. "Wahay Guru" is a mantra of ecstasy.

DOEI SHIVA KRIYA

Sit on your heels in Rock Pose. Raise your arms to a 60 degree angle with the hands bent at the wrists (FIGURE 8). Focus at the brow. Inhale in 16 parts and exhale in 16 parts. Keep the increments very minute so as to fit 16 distinct breaths into both the inhale and exhale. 3–31 minutes.

VISUALIZATION: With every "sniff" a little silver hammer is tapping your brow.

MODIFICATION: If you can't sit on your heels, cross your legs or sit in a chair.

FIGURE 8

This is a very sacred technique which helps to open your intuitive capacities and regenerate the glands. In Indian mythology, Shiva is considered the Lord of Yoga. It's said that he had to master 108 kinds of yoga over 108 eons, before he was granted the gift of Kundalini Yoga. Initially, this one's very difficult, but if you persevere you can build the time over time.

THOUGHT TRAINS

There are two thought trains
Inherent in the human,
To and from your City O my King,
May mine incline
Towards that that does illumine,
And may my life be the offering that I bring.

–Ravi Singh

SHEPHERD

I am my mind's shepherd
Among myriad hills.
Sometimes watching You
Most intensely
My thoughts do stray;
A hundred little winds ruffle
The waters
And the foxes come spying
From their dens.
Then I come back again
And to protect you O lambs
I sing to the fire
Long songs to the One we love;
And you are restless no longer
Not even of wolves,
Blessed are you to be soothed.

–Ravi Singh

CHAPTER 14

MASTER MEDITATIONS

THE MYSTERY OF MIND

Sages and wise men from the very beginning have wrestled with questions such as: "Where do thoughts come from?" "Do thoughts create our reality or does our reality create thoughts?" and "What is the mechanism for insight, intuition, and genius?" I'm sure you've thought about your mind. The problem is, trying to figure out the workings of the mind by thinking about it is like asking a Government Agency to investigate itself. Meditation will help you see and know things in and around you as they are, not as you think they are.

THOUGHT WAVES

According to Yoga: If our minds are to be considered oceans, then our thoughts are waves. When not in a state of Yoga (conscious balance), we unconsciously identify with thoughts and lose awareness of our True Selves.

Our Intellects select waves from an ocean of impulses and we become aware of certain thoughts. These thoughts manifest through a weather pattern (the vicissitudes of our lives) and can become a storm (our emotions) which batters the sea wall of our relationships and responsibilities.

When we combine finite motives with emotions, a desire is born. To extend the metaphor, desire can become a hurricane (a cycle of unconscious activity around our identity) which destroys everything in its path.

It's not that we're not aware of the Truth in us. The trouble is, we've been conditioned to place instant gratification on a pedestal and ignore the promptings of Creative Intelligence to seek the safety of high ground.

THREE MINDS

All of the above is compounded by the fact that the mind is multifaceted, consisting of different factions, at times diametrically opposed. Every time we think yes, another part of us simultaneously thinks no. This is the vicious cycle which keeps the average person in a constant state of confusion or conflict.

Yoga recognizes three aspects of the mind: Positive, Negative, and Neutral. The Positive Mind is our optimistic impulse. The Negative Mind deals in worst case scenarios to protect us. The Neutral Mind sees both sides equally, and offers the option best for us overall.

The Neutral (Non-Discriminating) Mind is not a given. It has to be developed through Meditation. Meditation helps us cultivate an overview to decide the best course to take in our Higher Self's best interest.

THE GREAT SECRET

Are you ready? Make sure no one's reading over your shoulder (just kidding). This is the Great Secret, the Meaning of Life: You can be president or pauper, CEO or hobo–it doesn't matter. Whatever you make sacred is the meaning of life. As Yogi Bhajan put it so eloquently: "It's not the life you lead; it's the Courage (and the sacredness) you bring to it."

A prerequisite for sacredness is commitment. Many people live by the maxim: "If it feels good, do it" and, by logical extension, "When the thrill is gone, do something else." This constant quest for sensation becomes an excuse for not moving forward.

It's not a person, place, or thing we commit to. As aspirants seeking to be humanly human and Divinely inspired, we want to learn to commit to commitment itself, and having done so, be willing to die before we fall. This mental attitude gives us tremendous personal power.

In a life without sacredness (commitment), emotion becomes a neurosis. Through the process of meditation as a tool for sacredness, we are able to turn emotion into devotion. Devotion fuels commitment (one-pointedness of mind). With our minds as one-pointed as lasers, we can cut through the haze of all extraneous concern and reflect our inner light off the mirror of Infinity so it can illuminate the world. Thus, our Destiny is served and all beings benefit.

How to Meditate

Do each meditation with attention to detail. If you do have lapses in your concentration, don't waste time feeling guilty, just bring yourself back to the task at hand and do your best with no thought of failure or reward. Use your creativity to bring meaning and power to the technique.

There are literally thousands of meditations. Each one addresses a certain facet of us. Overall, as stated, meditation helps us train our minds. We want to hold the stallion of our passions in the corral of consciousness and saddle it with Spirit, so that life can be an exhilarating ride across the prairie of wildflowers, and death a leap over the cliff where time and space give way to Grace.

Hotline

One of these days
We will turn a corner
Into a Light
Unknown to us now;
One of these days
We will turn a corner
And enter the Transparent World,
And I am listening
To your Voice
At this stage
Of the preceedings
When Spring rehearses
With lilacs of pure sound,
Listening to the round
Of soft waterfalls
As I breathe your Name
Over and again,
Lying in bed
With shrapnel in the heart,
Writing these words
With a blue pen,
Listening to your Voice
Of a thousand petals unfold–
Every time I call you answer.

–Ravi Singh

LONG EK ONG KARS

This important and powerful meditation can take you all the way. Where? To that place where your every thought and deed resonate at the frequency of Truth. Liberated beings live not for was/is but for Now On. Their behavior is always consistent with an inner experience, which is ecstasy beyond words.

Long Ek Ong Kars is a self-initiation into the mysteries of Self, towards self-liberation. In the tradition of Kundalini Yoga, we don't rely on someone else to touch us on the forehead or supply a magic pill to give us the experience of Spirit. We have the power to empower ourselves. We don't need mind readers; we should read our own minds. We don't need spiritualists; we should invoke our own Spirits.

Sit in Easy Pose with the spine straight. Your hands are in Gyan Mudra. Focus at the Third Eye or at the tip of the nose with your eyes ¹/₁₀ open, looking down (FIGURE 1). We're going to use the mantra:

- ◇ Inhale deeply and chant "Ek" (pulling the navel in slightly for emphasis; feeling the sound at the rectum). Then chant "Ong" (in a very nasal manner, feeling the sound in the sex organ area), and "Kar" (feeling the sound in the navel area).

- ◇ Inhale again and chant "Sat" (feeling the sound at the sternum), a very long "Nam" drawing out the "A" sound (feeling the sound at the throat), and, with your very last bit of breath, chant "Siri" (feeling this at the Third Eye). The "R" in "Siri" is pronounced almost like a "D."

- ◇ Now take a half breath and chant "Wha" (feeling this sound at the top of the head) and "Hay Guru" (feeling this above the top of the head).

So, we're chanting this mantra in a 2¹/₂ breath cycle; On the first breath, "Ek Ong Kar," On the second breath, "Sat Nam Siri," then after a half breath, "Wah Hay Guru."

This mantra means:

THERE'S ONE CREATOR WHO IS YOUR TRUE IDENTITY
INDESCRIBABLE IS THAT WISDOM
THERE ARE NO WORDS FOR THIS ECSTASY

FIGURE 1

You may practice this meditation for as long as you'd like. Try it for 31 minutes after doing a Kundalini Yoga set, as your morning routine. It's said if you practice this meditation before sunrise, 2½ hours a day for 40 days, it will give you an experience which will be yours forever. This meditation is also very effective when you're experiencing a negative emotion. Simply chant at that frequency, i.e., angrily, sadly, lustfully, fearfully, etc. It works! If done in this way, the focus of the eyes is at the tip of the nose. According to Yoga, there are 84 energy points on the roof of the mouth. As the tip of tongue hits the upper palate in certain combinations, it triggers chemical and electrical reactions in the brain. Through the use of mantras, we are literally programming ourselves to attain and maintain the experience of Higher Consciousness.

MEDITATION FOR PROPHETIC INSIGHT & POWER OF THE WORD

Sit in a meditative position (FIGURE 2). The top teeth are locked firmly over the bottom teeth. The underside of the tongue presses against the roof of the mouth. The eyes are ¹/₁₀ open, looking down towards the tip of the nose. Apply neck lock. Your chin is pulled back like a soldier at attention.

As you look down, mentally project "Sa-Ta-Na-Ma" continuously out the Third Eye, at a moderate pace. Look towards the tip of the nose and, concentrating up, feel a pressure in the Third Eye area. Do this meditation for at least 15 minutes, ideally 31 minutes or more. For the full experience of this technique, try 90 minutes.

FIGURE 2

This is called Drib Dhristi Lochina Karma Kriya, which means the Action of Acquiring Insight into Future Thought Forms. Usually mastery of a technique means to accrue the full range of benefits and have a definitive inner experience. This can take months or years. This is one of the rare techniques which can be mastered in one or several sittings if you really apply yourself. Here are some of the traditional claims for this meditation: You will be able to heal someone just by looking at them. You will have the Power of the Word, the ability to speak powerfully, poetically, and penetratingly, to express the Truth in any given situation; you will be able to project your magnetic influence anywhere, and know the outcome of any sequence of events you initiate. This meditation is most powerful when practiced on the eve of a full moon. At that time the glands are in an optimum state of readiness to secrete and balance you, and your subconscious can release mental impurities. It's said that if you practice this for 3 hours honestly, it will open up your psychic abilities.

BREATH MEDITATION TO MAKE YOU A HEALER

Your elbows are at the base of the ribs. The forearms angle up so that the hands meet at sternum level. The right hand is over the left, palms facing up, fingers slightly angled inward, thumbs stretched to the sides (FIGURE 3). Your eyes are closed.

Inhale and hold the breath, visualizing white light around the hands. Pull the navel in and mentally chant "Har Har Wahay Guru," holding the breath as long as you can. Exhale forcefully and visualize lightning shooting from the hands. 31 minutes.

FIGURE 3

This is called Sidh Karm Kriya. A Siddhi is a spiritual power granted through self-discipline. This meditation will give you the power to heal through touch and heal at a distance. The ability to take away pain is the first power granted to a Saint. This meditation also helps to evaporate inner anger. After 120 days of practice, you'll begin to feel heat building in your hands. Let us never forget, we are not the ones doing the healing, it's God working through us. Har is the Creative Aspect of the Infinite. Wahay Guru is the Experience of Ecstasy That Takes You from Darkness to Light.

MEDITATION TO BALANCE, BLESS & PROTECT YOU

This meditation is very powerful when practiced in conjunction with the previous one. It's very powerful on its own, as well. As in the previous meditation, we'll be using the mantra Har Har Wahay Guru.

Sit in a comfortable, meditative position (FIGURE 4). Inhale in four parts as you turn your head either way twice; i.e., take four successive inhales as you turn your head left, right, left, right. Then face forward and chant "Har Har Wahay Guru" five times at a moderate pace. Then take another four-part inhale and continue.

As you chant "Har," your mouth is open, as if in a ¾ yawn. With each "Har," pull your navel in slightly for emphasis. Place each of the five repetitions at the places in the body which correspond to the first five centers: rectum, sex organ, navel, sternum, and throat. The time for this one is open. Try it for 31, or better yet, 62 minutes.

FIGURE 4

This meditation will balance the five elements in you, a key to mastery and mental and physical health on all levels. In addition, this meditation will make you intuitive and keep you on the right path. You'll find it's easy to do this one for long periods of time. Build up to 2½ hours commencing before first light. This sun of your Spirit will illuminate the dawn.

MEDITATION TO RECONCILE & CLEANSE YOUR PAST

Your eyes are ¹/₁₀ open, looking down at the tip of the nose. One hand is over the other, away from the body at the level of the sternum (FIGURE 5). Take a few minutes to go into a deep meditative state. Then chant:

This mantra of Creativity and Regeneration translates as:

EXISTENCE, LIFE, DEATH, AND REBIRTH

Feel the consonants S, T, N, and M, of "Sa, Ta, Na, Ma," coming in through the top of the head, the "A" sound going out the brow. This is called the "L" form.

Chant for 15–31 minutes, then inhale, hold the breath, press the underside of the tongue against the roof of the mouth, turn your eyes up, and hear the echo of your chanting in your mind. Relax the breath and hand position and meditate for 11 minutes. If you see scenes, or have a thought, feeling, or emotion from your past, mentally release it to Infinity.

FIGURE 5

Who we are is not who we were, it's who we were born to be. If we walk down the street facing backwards, we're bound to hurt ourselves. This meditation will begin to free you from the haunting experiences and patterns which continuously engender pain. This meditation will put you in a surprisingly deep state. Take time afterwards to come back to earth before resuming normal activity.

THE MUSIC OF HEAVEN

And you created
A temple for them
Deep inside their ears.

–Rilke

Music and sound represent a potent and graceful inner technology, and are very important components of Kundalini Yoga and the tradition it comes out of. A powerful and enjoyable Meditation consists of chanting any of the various mantras we use. There are a number of inspiring tapes you can purchase to further beautify this process (see Appendix 3).

I Belong to You and No Other

◇

When I think your Name we rhyme;
An angel is born on that breath.
May my prayer be
That I manifest a Destiny.
In the window of my psyche
I see a throne,
Reserved for You alone.
I know and shall believe
That the remembrance of You
Is a reprieve from all suffering;
For if blessings occur
It is by your Grace
And adversity's bitter pill
Is by your will.
O Diver,
As an oyster is pearled
So too steal me
From this dark and heavy water
Into the daylight
Where I shall adorn You.
You are the lover of the lonely,
The inamorata of all my days,
The ways and means
Of all who attempt greatness,
The one way through this maze
Of thunder
Where the walls are skulls—
Magnetic Master, Solar Friend,
It is the end of procrastination,
Your lovers are a nation
Of celebration and discipline.
I am a wave of Infinity
Briefly awash on the shore of time.
Soon the ocean of light
Will gently and inexorably
Reclaim me
And you will meet me at the altar
And rename me.

–Ravi Singh

DAILY DISCIPLINE

Rise before the sun
Acquires enough leverage
To foreclose on the dark hours;
Breathe that rare air
Sleep and revelers
Are not sanctioned for;
Chant the Nomenclature of the Unknown
And its corollary sobriquets;
Calm yourself, strengthen yourself,
Love yourself;
Go out into the day refortified
And heal the world.
Keep your appointment with the Timeless One;
Even manic isotopes pause to praise Him.
Cross the desert in the hourglass
The hand of fate turns on a whim.

–Ravi Singh

WHY I TEACH YOGA

◆

I am seeing art in the dark–
When the lights go on
They fan themselves with programs
And stare at red curtains
Descended from a secret sky.
Beautifully conditioned dancers
Described the contours of evening.
Perfect performance–
But the audience looks and leaves
The same.
We need something to transform us
A lever, a Lover,
A Reality we never knew.

–Ravi Singh

CHAPTER 15

⎯⎯⎯⎯◇◆◇⎯⎯⎯⎯

THE KEY TO VICTORY
& THE HIGHEST VOCATION

THE KEY TO VICTORY—SADHANA

Sadhana means daily discipline. Discipline means doing your practice even when you feel least like doing it. Anyone can do deep breathing for an hour and feel "spiritual," but to attain and maintain Higher Consciousness requires a day-to-day process.

A discipline dictates we commit consciously and subconsciously to our Higher Selves; otherwise we're constantly flirting with ourselves. With this discipline, the energy of Kundalini, Spirit becomes the driving force in our lives. It is not limited by time, space, personality, or death.

The most powerful time for doing Sadhana is before sunrise. Among those of us who've made Kundalini Yoga a way of life, we try to make Sadhana a community affair. Doing it on your own is, of course, great as well.

It's easy to see the need to take a shower every morning. Most of us were never taught that we have to cleanse our subconscious minds daily as well. Otherwise, we invariably experience arguments and turmoil as subconscious pollution causes us to hurt ourselves and others and to consistently make wrong decisions.

There are some very cogent reasons for doing Sadhana before sunrise. According to Oriental healing systems, specific energy flows in the body are most active at certain times. The Lung Meridians are most open between 3 and 5 a.m., making it a propitious and healthy time to breathe consciously.

In the quiet hours before dawn, the so-called "psychic airwaves" are most clear. All the frenetic activity of the day hasn't started yet. Many spiritual traditions have recognized the early morning hours as conducive to meditation.

It's said that the guiding, protective, and magnetic influences of the great Saints and Sages of the Ages are most accessible in the early pre-dawn hours.

Sleeping after sunrise makes our breathing very shallow. This triggers very weird and often disturbing dreams which can sap our energy and lessen the probability of having a great day.

For the average person, dreaming is the filtering mechanism for subconscious stress. The heaviest dreaming usually occurs around the dawn hours. Dreams are extremely stressful on our nervous systems. Sadhana is a much more elegant, effective, and complete way of keeping our subconscious clean.

Practicing Kundalini Yoga and Meditation in the early morning hours helps us in the following ways: Our circulatory systems are stimulated, our lungs are expanded, our magnetic fields are charged, our muscles are strengthened, our lymphatic systems are circulated, our nervous systems are cleared, our glandular systems are balanced, our navel points are centered; Also, our sense of self is expanded to include the Higher Self, our lives are synced to the rhythm of life, our subconscious minds are cleansed, and our souls are celebrated. Not a bad way to start the day! The general model for Sadhana is 45 minutes to 1 hour of Kundalini Yoga followed by chanting six mantras for 11 minutes each.

As a conscious person committed to working on yourself, and based on everything I've said, can you think of any reason not to do Sadhana? When confronted with a decision or activity requiring a leap of faith, this is a very good bottom-line equation: In the greater scheme of things, can you think of any reason not to do it?

If getting up at 4 a.m. and doing Kundalini Yoga and Meditation seems too extreme for you, you can start by getting up 1/2 hour earlier and doing 15 minutes of yoga and 15 minutes of meditation. Keep building up the times and pushing the time back from there.

Our egos, the limiting factor within us, love to sleep. Our souls never sleep. When you get up to do Sadhana, you're honoring your soul. When you consciously commit to the life of the soul, you will be surprisingly happy. When we sacrifice our time and space (to get up early and work on ourselves), time and space serve us.

See page 149 for information on ordering a tape of Sadhana chants.

The Highest Vocation—A Teacher's Manifesto

By the time you're reading this, I hope you've experienced the beauty and power of Kundalini Yoga and Meditation. I'm sure you can think of many people in your life who can benefit from this work right off the bat. Consider asking any interested parties to participate the next time you do a set. When you're confident you can present these techniques in a responsible manner, take it a step further. Offer a formal class.

In a planetary sense, we're in a state of transition. Everything is in flux. The Universe is crying out for a few good people to heal, uplift, and inspire. Out of gratitude for what this work has given you, share it with all. For information on formal Teacher Training, see Appendix 5. Based on Yogi Bhajan's—my Teacher's—impeccable example, I have compiled the following guidelines for teaching Kundalini Yoga:

◇ If you want to master something, teach it.

◇ Never teach anything you've never done yourself.

◇ Seek to deliver your students—not to you, but beyond you.

◇ When a student asks for information or clarification never say, "I don't know." Either do the research or direct them to someone who can answer their question.

◇ Do your discipline. The further you can take yourself, the further you can take others.

◇ Never ever use students' trust in you to serve yourself. In ancient yogic texts it says, "Whosoever exploits a student will be reborn as a cockroach or worm!"

◇ Seek to speak God's Truth, not circumstantial truth.

◇ The Universe will test you through your students. Stay righteous and treat everyone equally.

◇ Train your students to be Teachers in their own right, and to strive to be 10 times better than you. The Universe needs people to put their bodies on the line to be Divine and to heal, uplift, and inspire others.

◇ Never compromise yourself by looking to a student for any kind of emotional or sexual gratification. Assume that you will be tested in this manner. Turn emotion into Devotion, and lust into Desire to be higher!

◇ Know that sometimes the most beautiful souls come to you in the most unlikely vehicles (bodies).

◇ Don't play favorites and don't play God.

◇ Always remember that the path of a Teacher of Truth is one of the most meritorious and noble of all endeavors.

◇ The Universe has a timetable for the development of each of us. Don't try to force people to take a step they're not ready for. At the same time, always inspire people to take the next step on the path they're on, even if it means losing them as a student. Ten more will come to take their place.

◇ It's important that you give students the privilege of returning energy (money) for the energy they've received.

◇ Consider giving 10% of your teaching income back to the source of the teachings or to some other worthy cause.

◇ Don't pass your limitations on to your students.

◇ Accommodate everyone at their own level of understanding.

◇ Be yourself and use the gifts God gave you to enhance your teaching.

◇ Be willing to go anywhere to heal, uplift, inspire, and share, but don't feel you have to save the world all by yourself. As a general rule, teach in the circumstances you enjoy most.

◇ As a Teacher, continue to take classes yourself, to get new ideas and regenerate.

◇ At the end of each class, consider taking a few moments to pray or project for Peace.

A TEACHER'S SONG

The Spiritual Master arrives
And bows before the beginning student.
Try to live to see this!

–Kabir

People come to Yoga class
With an undefined longing
Culled from the travelposters
Of an inner need.
Despite appearances
Some get immediate clearance
For takeoff to a Destiny;
And I am blessed to be witness
To the emergence
Of these butterfly souls,
Triggered by Love's lightning,
In fields of the Equinox,
Redolent with the fragrance of God.

–Ravi Singh

THE CHAKRAS

*T*he Chakras are fountains of energy that lie along the spine. Each Chakra represents an aspect of consciousness, mode of behavior, or perspective, and is an etheric counterpart of an important nerve center or gland. Your understanding of this model will enable you to assess where you are on the path of self-growth, and help others accordingly. There are eight major Chakras. When our energy is flowing freely through all of them, we can easily be complete and fulfilled.

THE FIRST CHAKRA

The First Chakra is at the rectum. Its frequency corresponds to the color red, and its quality to the element earth. This center relates to elimination, instinct, survival, and habits, and represents the realm of the quotidian, ordinary day-to-day life. When our energy is flowing freely through this center, we are grounded, dependable, realistic, and secure. If energy is stuck here, there's a tendency to be clinging, coarse, overly stubborn, and exhibit signs of an addictive or anal-retentive personality. A first center imbalance can also manifest as very ungrounded or spacey behavior. The First Chakra holds subconscious patterns. Neurotic or perverse behavior and deep insecurities are examples of first center imbalances.

THE SECOND CHAKRA

The Second Chakra is a nerve center in the area of the sex organ. Its frequency corresponds to the color orange, and its quality is that of water. It is the realm of sensation. When energy is flowing freely through this center, a person is expressive, balanced in relationship, and has a personal flair and a sense of individuality. If energy is stuck at the Second Chakra, one tends to be overly-obsessed with sex and its cultural accoutrements, or overly puritanical in relation to it.

THE THIRD CHAKRA

The Third Chakra corresponds to the Navel Point/solar plexus area. Its frequency corresponds to saffron-yellow, and its quality is that of fire. It is the seat of power, and is a reservoir for the energy of life.

When energy is flowing freely through this center, a person is focused and fearless. He or she has a strong will and is successful in life. When the energy is blocked here, a person tends to exploit others or is too easily exploited. There is also a tendency to be drunk on emotions, intensity, passion, or power.

The first three centers, or "Lower Triangle," relate to the mind, our patterns, and persuasions. The higher centers relate to the Spirit and higher potential. Ideally, the lower centers supply a base or framework for the experience of the higher.

THE FOURTH CHAKRA

The fourth center is called the Heart Center. It lies in the area of the sternum. Its frequency corresponds to the color green and its quality to the element air. It relates to love, expansion, and the indefatigable nature of the human spirit.

When the Heart Center is open, you begin to get a sense of your Infinite identity. You have the capacity to sacrifice for the sake of sacrifice, and love unqualifiedly. The Heart Center is the first center of higher consciousness.

An imbalance at the Heart Center often renders a person incapable of saying no; in other words, they overextend themselves, or feel overwhelmed by their feelings. It may also result in hardheartedness, lack of compassion, and manic behavior.

THE FIFTH CHAKRA

The fifth center is the Throat Center, which is related to the thyroid gland. Its frequency corresponds to the color light blue and its quality to the element ether. Through the Throat Center we give substance to idea. It is the seat of creativity. When energy is flowing through the Throat Center, we can speak eloquently, command, translate our concepts into reality, speak the truth and live the truth. When the Throat Center is blocked, we feel creatively stifled, and have difficulty being direct and truthful in our dealings with others.

The Sixth Chakra

The sixth center, at the brow, is called the Third Eye or Ajna Chakra. Its frequency relates to the color indigo. Its quality is beyond quality. Through the sixth center, we master our minds and pierce the veil of illusion. Our awareness here is focus itself. The Third Eye corresponds to the pituitary gland.

When the Third Eye is in balance, we have a meditative mind, the ability to know the Unknown, see the Unseen, and an understanding of our Destiny.

The Seventh Chakra

The seventh center, at the top of the head, is called the Thousand-Petalled Lotus, or the Seat of the Soul. Its relative frequency corresponds to the color violet. It relates to the pineal gland. When the seventh center is in balance, we feel part of the vastness of all that is. The experience here is ecstasy beyond words.

The Eighth Chakra

The eighth center, above the top of the head, is your Aura, and represents the working balance of all the centers; our ability to integrate Higher Consciousness into our presence and projection.

◆◇◆

THE TEN BODIES

*T*he model of the Ten Bodies is an archetype that describes the aspects of our totality in a multidimensional sense. When the ten bodies are completely formed and are working in unison, they are merged and form the eleventh body, which represents the perfected being.

THE SOUL BODY

The first spiritual body is the Soul Body. This body represents our very essence, uncomplicated and pure. It's that quiet but insistent inner voice that inspires us towards God.

When we refuse to recognize the promptings of our soul, we find ourselves embroiled in conflicts between our head and heart. Sometimes we have to circumvent "reason" to give sustenance to our soul.

THE NEGATIVE MIND

The second spiritual body is called the Negative Mind, and it helps us calculate possible pitfalls in any given situation. People whose Negative Minds are not in balance frequently find themselves giving away their power, out of a tremendous need to connect with others in various kinds of relationships.

To master our second body, we must be able to transform emotion into Devotion. In other words, we have to choose to "fall in love" with the things which will never let us down, i.e., Yoga, the guidance of a True Teacher who inspires us to Infinity, a path with heart, and God and His Grand Design.

THE POSITIVE MIND

The third spiritual body is called the Positive Mind, and it relates to our optimistic aspect, the ability to give hope to all. When our positive minds are imbalanced, we tend to be negative and depressed, void of hope.

THE NEUTRAL MIND

The fourth spiritual body is called the Neutral Mind. The Neutral Mind is not a given, but has to be developed through meditation. It represents the ability to see both sides of every issue and arrive at the course of action or insight which is in our overall best interest. The Neutral (Non-Discriminating) Mind is one of the highest attainments in Yoga. It leads to Liberation.

THE PHYSICAL BODY

The fifth spiritual body is the Physical Body. In the ultimate sense, people who master this aspect are able to sacrifice their comfort, well being, safety–even their lives–to lead others to an experience of Infinity. This is the domain of a true Teacher. When a person's fifth body is not integrated, he/she can be indulgent and lazy. The remedy is movement. Exercise, dance, walk, run, and above all, do Kundalini Yoga!

THE ARCLINE

The sixth body is called the Arcline. It relates to the beaming power of your mind, the ability to project to Infinity and get a corresponding readout in reality. This is the power of prayer. When the Arcline is strong, a person is intuitive, focused, and successful. When one's Arcline is weak, a person tends to be scattered and accident-prone.

THE MAGNETIC FIELD

The seventh body is the Magnetic Field. When this is strong, you have the ability to heal, uplift, and inspire by your very presence. You have charisma. When your Magnetic Field is weak, you tend to repel rather than attract people, and frequently feel overlooked and anonymous. People with weak auras have a greater tendency to be in the wrong place at the wrong time.

THE PRANIC BODY

The eighth body is called the Pranic Body, and relates to energy and fearlessness. When it's strong, you have the ability to regenerate very effectively and keep going. All forms of Yogic breathing which we practice in Kundalini Yoga activate the Pranic Body. Remember: When you master your breathing, you master your mind. The Pranic Body feeds in through the adrenals. When the Pranic Body is strong, you have the ability to get "jazzed up," and impart energy to all those around you.

THE SUBTLE BODY

The ninth body is called the Subtle Body and it relates to Mastery; the ability to know the Unknown and see the Unseen, to read between the lines, and see beneath the surface. When our Subtle Body is not integrated, we tend to be very insensitive, awkward, and somewhat scattered. To develop the Subtle Body, we must learn to be sensitive to our sensitivity. Yogis tell us that the Subtle Body is the capsule which conveys the soul to its Destination at the time of Death.

THE RADIANT BODY

The tenth body is called the Radiant Body. It relates to nerve strength, royal courage, and the ability to stand out and take a stand. The Radiant Body is our warrior aspect–all or nothing.

THE ELEVENTH BODY

The eleventh body, as stated before, is the crystallization of the ten bodies. To bring this about, one must transcend one's narrowness, dedicate oneself to a path with heart, and "Bow before the Word of God."

KUNDALINI YOGA MANTRAS

Most of the mantras which follow were not presented in this book, but constitute an important part of Kundalini Yoga. If you continue your practice through our teaching centers, or obtain some of the additional books or tapes we offer, no doubt you'll encounter some of these.

Ad Guray Nameh, Jugad Guray Nameh,
Sat Guray Nameh, Siri Guru Dev A Nameh
I bow to the Primal Wisdom, I bow to the Wisdom through the Ages,
I bow to the True Wisdom, I bow to the great Unseen Wisdom.

Ang Sung Wahay Guru
My every molecule dances to the music of God.

Ap Sahaee Hoa, Such A Da Such A Doa, Har, Har, Har,
I take refuge in the True One, the True One is my True Support, God, God, God.

Ardas Bayee, Amar Das Guru, Amar Das Guru,
Ardas Bayee, Ram Das Guru, Ram Das Guru,
Ram Das Guru, Suchee Sahee
The fulfillment of your prayers is guaranteed by the Grace of Guru Amar Das
(The Hope for the Hopeless) and Guru Ram Das (King of the Yogis and Bestower
of Blessings), Past, Present, and Future, Signed, Sealed, and Delivered.

Ek Ong Kar, Sat Nam, Siri Wahay Guru
There is One Creator, Who is your
True Identity, That Wisdom is Great
and Indescribable.

Ek Ong Kar, Sat Nam, Karta Purkh, Near Bhao, Nir Vair,
Akal Moort, Ajuni, Sai Bhung, Gur Prasad, Jap, Ad Such, Jugad Such,
Habee Such, Nanaka Hosee Bee Such
There's One Creator, Whose Name is Truth, the Doer of Everything, Fearless,
Revengeless, Undying, Unborn, and Self-Illumined; This is revealed through
the True Guru's Grace—Meditate! True in the beginning, True through the ages,
True now, O Nanak, the True One shall ever be True.

Gobinday, Mukunday, Udaray, Uparay, Hariang,
Kariang, Near Nomay, Akamay
Sustainer, Liberator, Enlightener, Infinite, Destroyer,
Creator, Nameless, Desireless.

Ong Namo Guru Dev Namo
Infinite Creative Consciousness, I call on you;
Divine Wisdom Within, I call on you.

Rakay Rakanahara Ap Ubarian, Gurki Paya Pairee Paii Kaj Savarian,
Ho Apa Diaya Manoh Na Visarian, Sadha Jana Kai Sanga Bhavjala Tarian, Sakata
Nindaka Dushta Khin Mah Bidarian, Tisa Sahiba Ki Tayka Nanaka Mania
Mah, Jis Simrat Sukh Hoe Sagala Dukh Jah, Jis Simrat Sukh Hoe Sagala Dukh Jah.
O Savior Lord: Save us all and take us across, uplifting and giving the excellence. You
gave us the touch of the lotus feet of the Guru and our works are embellished with perfection.
You are Merciful, Kind, and Compassionate and our minds do not forget You.
In the Company of the Holy, You save us from misfortune. You destroy the enemies of the
Pure Ones in a moment. The Lord Master is my anchor and support. O Nanak,
hold firm in my mind. Upon remembering Him, Bliss wells up in me and all pain leaves.

Sat Nam
True Identity.

Sa Ta Na Ma
Existence, Life, Death, & Rebirth.

Sat Narien, Wahay Guru, Haree Narien, Sat Nam
*Clear Perception of Truth, Indescribable Wisdom, Clear Perception of the Creative
Essence of the Divine, True Identity.*

Wahay Guru
Ecstasy Beyond Words.

Wha Yantay, Kar Yantay, Juga Duta Patee, Adaka Ita Whaha,
Brahmaday, Taysha Guru, Ita Whahay Guru
*Great Macroself, Creative Self, All that is Creative through time,
All that is the Great One, Generating, Organizing and Destroying, contained
in the experience of Ecstasy Beyond Words.*

Guru Guru Wahay Guru, Guru Ram Das Gur
The Wisdom which comes as a Servant of the Infinite.

Har
The Creative Aspect of Infinity.

Many of these mantras, as well as many other inspiring offerings, can be enjoyed
on tapes, with musical accompaniment. There are also other instructional materials
available. For a free catalog, write:

G.T. International
1800 S. Robertson Suite 182
Los Angeles, CA 90035
(213) 551-0484

Golden Temple Recordings
8829 Pickford St.
Los Angeles, CA 90035
(213) 274-0963

THE ULTIMATE KEY TO
STRENGTH, SUCCESS & SPIRIT

Elevate yourself and others.

–Yogi Bhajan

◦◇◦

KUNDALINI YOGA
TEACHING CENTERS

No matter where you live on Planet Earth, chances are that Kundalini Yoga classes are given somewhere near.

Some of our activities include Summer and Winter Solstice yoga retreats, special seminars worldwide, as well as a host of regional classes and services. The 3HO Foundation, which is comprised of Kundalini Yoga Teachers and Centers, is the largest accredited Yoga Teachers' Organization in the world.

For more information on our programs and Teacher Training, please contact one of the following:

3HO Foundation
International Headquarters
P.O. Box 351149
Los Angeles, CA 90035
(213) 552-3415

Ravi Singh/Kundalini Yoga
c/o White Lion Press
225 E. 5th St. #4D
New York, NY 10003
(212) 475-0212

Kundalini Yoga Centers
Gurucharan Singh Khalsa
18 Grove St.
Wellesley, MA 02161
(617) 237-5872

3HO Superhealth
Yoga Vacation & Detox
2545 N. Woodland Ave
Tucson, AZ 85719
(602) 749-0404

MIX & MATCH
GROUP A

SEQUENCE 1

SEQUENCE 2

SEQUENCE 3

SEQUENCE 4

*Practice one or more of these Sequences in order as a warm-up for the
Sets/Meditations in Chapters 7–14 and/or move to the next page.*

MIX & MATCH
GROUP B

SEQUENCE 1

SEQUENCE 2

SEQUENCE 3

SEQUENCE 4

*Practice one or more of these Sequences in order as a warm-up for the
Sets/Meditations in Chapters 7–14 and/or move to the next page.*

MIX & MATCH
GROUP C

SEQUENCE 1

SEQUENCE 2

SEQUENCE 3

 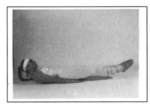 

SEQUENCE 4

Practice one or more of these Sequences in order as a warm-up for the
Sets/Meditations in Chapters 7–14 and/or move to the next page.

MIX & MATCH
GROUP D

SEQUENCE 1

SEQUENCE 2

SEQUENCE 3

SEQUENCE 4

Practice one or more of these Sequences in order as a warm-up for the
Sets/Meditations in Chapters 7–14 and/or move to the next page.

MIX & MATCH
GROUP E

SEQUENCE 1

SEQUENCE 2

SEQUENCE 3

SEQUENCE 4

*Practice one or more of these Sequences in order as a warm-up for the
Sets/Meditations in Chapters 7–14 and/or move to the next page.*

MIX & MATCH
GROUP F

SEQUENCE 1

SEQUENCE 2

SEQUENCE 3

SEQUENCE 4

*Practice one or more of these Sequences in order as a warm-up for the
Sets/Meditations in Chapters 7–14.*

ABOUT YOGI BHAJAN

Yogi Bhajan is the acknowledged Master of Kundalini and White Tantric Yogas. He came to the United States in 1969 and founded the Healthy, Happy, Holy (3HO) Organization, which has now expanded to over 100 Teaching Centers worldwide, including the Soviet Union.

Yogi Bhajan is the author of: *The Teachings of Yogi Bhajan, The Ancient Art of Self-Nutrition, Romance & Reality,* and *The Mind & Its Intrigues,* among many other books. A large variety of Kundalini Yoga and Meditation manuals have been published to transmit his teachings.

Yogi Bhajan's integrity and Mastery have inspired people from all walks of life. His main motivation is to empower people to blossom and bring hope and healing to a world in transition.

He has said, "I'm not here to gather disciples, but to train Teachers to be ten times better than me." And "I don't initiate people into Higher Consciousness, I teach them to initiate themselves."

As of this writing, Yogi Bhajan teaches on a regular basis in Los Angeles and in New Mexico. For information on his teaching schedule, call (213) 552-3416.

YOGI BHAJAN

ABOUT THE AUTHOR

Ravi Singh is putting yoga on the map! For the past 19 years in and around New York City and nationwide, he's been teaching in many diverse contexts: from scientists at Bell Labs in New Jersey, to opera singers at the Aspen Music festival, from inmates of prisons, to backstage with the stars of Broadway plays.

His clients have included such notables as Liv Ullmann, Yehudi Menuhin, Adrienne Vittadini, and Tina Louise, among others. The Yoga Teachers' Alliance (White Plains, New York) has called him the Teachers' Teacher.

ALSO BY RAVI SINGH:

BOOKS
Long Song to the One I Love
$7.95 (poetry; 70 pages)

Kundalini Yoga for Body, Mind, & Beyond
$15.95 (beautifully illustrated; 215 pages)

VIDEOS
Kundalini Yoga with Ravi Singh
(60 min.) $28.95

Ultimate Stretch/Warrior Workout
(90 min.) $29.95

The Kundalini Experience
(60 min.) $29.95

Send your order plus $2 shipping and handling to:

WHITE LION PRESS
225 E. 5th St. #4D
New York, New York 10003

A PRAYER

Your Light
Is a beauteous benediction;
Its legal tender
Is the unification
Of all suns, all worlds.
You are the origin
And outcome of all Yoga,
The Bestower of Breath.
May the Gifts of Grace we accrue
Be employed
To serve and honor You.
May we be inspired
To sow the seeds of Spirit
In your Name.
May our prayer be to blend
With your Aspects
And Excellences forever.
May the adoration
Of your Name never cease.
May Perfect Peace,
Abundance, Life,
Redemption, Healing,
Forgiveness,
Expansion,
And Understanding
Be granted
Unto all mankind.
May these Teachings be preserved
With reverence
And may the Experience
Of Spirit
Heal, uplift, and inspire all.
Sat Nam.